Coach

Coach

Terry Prone Tells It Like It Is

Terry Prone

First published in 2013

by Londubh Books

18 Casimir Avenue, Harold's Cross, Dublin 6w, Ireland

www.londubh.ie

1 3 5 4 2

Origination by Londubh Books; cover by bluett

Cover photo by Robbie Reynolds Photography

Printed by ScandBook AB, Falun, Sweden

ISBN: 978-1-907535-32-1

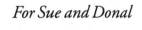

For Sue and Donal

A8

Contents

Introduction

Coaching is the hidden bit of my business. We've always trained people to make presentations, appear on television, handle meetings and write reports. We've always been known for providing PR advice to companies, individuals and political parties. We manage crisis communications when a company blows itself up, literally or figuratively. That's the front-of-house part of our work.

And then, there's coaching, where someone who wants to go far decides that they need someone outside their own family or their own business to help them develop their skills, hone their approach or soften their edges, in order to reach their personal goals. Or it can be a company that spots a potential winner and commissions us to work with that individual over, say, a six-month period or a year in order to help them develop.

Most of the time, coaching has a positive objective but, on occasion, the catalyst is negative. The individuals themselves get the sense that they're not waving but drowning, not winning but losing. Or an executive is told by the person to whom they report that coaching is necessary to enable them to eliminate deficits revealed by an annual review.

It all depends. But the reason for coaching seriously influences the attitude the individual brings to the situation. Believing your job may be under threat means that you regard coaching as about as attractive as a suspended sentence with an electronic ankle-bracelet built in, whereas deciding off your own bat to seek external expertise means you enter the relationship nervously but with reasonably positive expectations.

A good coach doesn't want to own you or get your applause. They will be totally concentrated on you and they won't set out to find you in the wrong. Why would they? They should, however, spot the potholes in your road that can slow your progress, or, if hit with too much enthusiasm, wreck your undercarriage.

Some individuals are more likely to encounter one particular kind of pitfall than others. If, for example, you are a high energy person fascinated by new technology, if you are what Malcolm Gladwell called an 'early adopter' in his 2005 book, *Blink*, if you are surrounded by sources of incoming information, the obstacle to your success may be distractions and how well or how badly you cope with these distractions.

If, in contrast, you are a quiet, introverted and reflective person, the biggest obstacle to your career success may be your boss or your colleagues neither registering nor acknowledging all you have to offer, because they're more attuned to extroverts and accordingly may not notice you in any real way.

If you experience high stress, if you worry about work and don't have a sense that everything will work out happily for you, that very pessimism may be the factor that will get in the way of what you could otherwise achieve.

Coaching executives to success over the past twenty years has taught me to spot career pitfalls. Some are unique to one individual but many are more widely experienced. They pop up again and again, in marginally different forms. In fact, it's usually one of ten major pitfalls that stops promising careers in their path. That's where this book can help you. Each chapter is an account of an executive undergoing coaching, what they discovered about themselves and how they applied that – or failed to apply it – to ensure that they fulfilled their career ambitions.

I should make it clear that none of the case studies is actually a portrait of a real client. They are composites, based on observing hundreds of executives as they built their careers and coped with challenges. What I have done is take a frequently occurring career pothole and personify the issue using one character.

For this reason, you may gain most out of *Coach* by not reading it all at one go. Choose the career pitfall closest to your own experience and start there.

Each chapter, in addition to telling the story of one executive or entrepreneur, picks out the circumstances or personal traits that threaten their future and gives advice on how, if you share these circumstances or personal traits, you might manage them so they don't prove a drag to your progress at work. And the last chapter offers more about coaching itself.

1

The Man Who Lacked Drive

That was me in Cork airport, a new Jack Reacher in hand and a bag of Lily O'Brien's sticky toffees in my carry-on, opened so that I could oh-so-casually sneak them out, one at a time, during the hour that was in front of me before boarding. Minding my own business, I was, when this guy drops to his hunkers beside me. I nearly had a double cardiac infarction. I let a strangled scream out of me, tossed my coffee over Jack Reacher and my trousers, leaped to my feet to try to pull the scalding cloth away from my thighs, dropped my mobile phone, which split into its component parts, and overturned my carry-on, the handle of which narrowly avoided taking out a toddler who was stuck to the ground in shock. The man came up off his hunkers and retreated, palms up in the 'See, I'm unarmed and intend you no harm' gesture.

'Jasus, Mickey, that's the best tackle I ever saw you execute and it not even on the pitch,' an older man said, while he picked up the bits of my Blackberry, reassembled it and tested it. The coffee on my trousers was now cold and clingy and made me look incontinent. Jack Reacher hadn't fared well, either. He was bent and damp and coffee-stained. The toddler retrieved my coffee beaker and handed it to me as carefully as if it was full. I thanked her and apologised to her for frightening her. 'I give you a kiss,' she said affably and did so before her mother dragged her to a safer seat. The man who had caused it all grabbed tissues from the nearby coffee station and mopped up the floor. I wouldn't say we were back to normal but my heart had resumed its usual pace and the crowds of interested bystanders were dispersing. I sat down and looked up at him.

'Hello,' he said solemnly, which broke up the minority who had stayed to watch.

'Hello,' I said back and patted the chair beside me. 'Why don't you sit down?'

The older man returned my phone and fisted the bloke now sitting beside me in the upper arm.

'How's them knees?'

'Good. Say nuthin'.'

'Big ask.'

'We're up for it.'

The older man nodded and headed off to his flight. Mickey, beside me, got formal, offering a surname – let's say it was Donohoe – and a handshake so turbo-charged, I thought I'd be wearing a sling for a week. Just as the pain died down, three boys of about thirteen appeared, clutching bits of paper, and Mickey stood up again and gave them chat and an autograph.

'Am I the only person in this entire airport who doesn't know who the hell you are?' I asked as he sat down for the second time.

'I'm Mickey – '

'Donohoe. I know. But you're obviously famous for something. What is it?'

'Football.'

'Which kind?'

He began to laugh. 'GAA.'

'I'm sorry not to know who you are. My husband says he's married to a sporting illiterate.'

'No, it's great. I've been thinking for a while I should go up and see you and then when I spotted you it seemed a good time.'

'See me for what?'

'Sort me head out, careerwise.'

'Coaching sessions?'

'Exactly.'

I went searching in the carry-on for a card and scribbled Stephanie's name on it.

'If I make an appointment, I'll get it wrong or double-book with someone else and you'll end up mad at me. Ring Steph and she'll sort a date that'll stick.'

He nodded, rose, gave me another crushing handshake and departed. Or so I thought. Just as I got back to finding how Jack was doing after the external application of hot brown liquid, the big man reappeared, clutching a fresh coffee.

'Replacement,' he said, thrusting it at me. 'Sorry.'

I watched him retreating, wondering if I'd see him again. When someone yields to the temptation to accost you on impulse, the odds are 50/50 that you'll never hear from them again. But just a few days later, my husband, checking through the company's electronic calendar, muttered something about a contradiction in terms.

'Huh?'

'You're booked to see a man who shares a name with a very famous footballer.'

'Who?'

'Mickey Donohoe.'

'No, it *is* the footballer. I met him in the airport.'

'How did you know him?' Tom knows damn well that I would not be able to pick any footballer, past or present, David Beckham included, out of a police line-up.

'I didn't. He introduced himself to me. Seems a nice fella.'

'Except if you're in his path on the field,' Barry, one of our consultants, said. He and Tom got into a lengthy recollection of some match where my new friend Mickey had creamed some poor hoor from an opposing team, nearly breaking both his femurs, but not in any way dirty. My new friend Mickey seemed – from what I could learn by eavesdropping on the conversation of two evident fans – to be a clean player possessed of the stamina of a yak, the speed of a panther and the determination of a Sherman tank. Taller than most guys who play in that position, too.

'Why does he want to see you?' my husband asked. Barry instinctively nodded. No offence, the nod said, but how could you help this Croker star?

'I have no clue. Soon as he finds out my limitations, I'll hand him over to ye,' I promised. 'Behave yourselves in the meantime and I might even introduce him to the two of you.'

The day Mickey arrived, I encountered more of my colleagues, male and female, than ever before, in casual encounters on the stairs of the Old Synagogue. Every one of them seemed to want to run into the football star. Mickey Donohoe engaged with each of them, was funny, self-deprecatory and – dressed up in a suit as opposed to the tracksuit he'd worn at the airport – astonishingly good-looking.

'Have to tell you that some of my colleagues believe you picked a right woodener when you booked in to see me, as opposed to one of them, who'd know who you are and be properly reverential,' I told him. 'This bit's going to be tedious, because your story is common currency and you're probably sick of going through it. But tell me about yourself anyway.'

He was second-eldest of five children born to a county council worker and a primary school teacher. When he was six, playing ball with his older brother in the front garden, he kicked it straight through the big window in the sitting room, where his mother was sewing. He and his older brother hesitated before going into the house and just as they were about to open the door, it opened and his mother stood there.

'It was like a horror film. She was, I mean, blood was running down from here – ' he tapped his right temple ' – and from her arms and she was holding the dress she'd been working on and it was spattered with blood. I could see a V-shaped bit of glass sticking into her forearm like a dart. My older brother started babbling that it wasn't him, it wasn't him, and I started to cry and she just stood there bleeding. She looked at the dress for my sister in her hand – it was lavender, I hate that colour ever since – and kind of examined the blood all over it and then kind of dropped it as if it had got too heavy. I was expecting her to drop beside it and die. And then she began to laugh. I swear to God, she stood there, bleeding all over, and laughed like someone had told her the funniest joke. After a while she shook her head and she pointed at my brother. 'Blue basin, boiled water, Dettol. Three parts water to one part Dettol and don't add to the excitement by scalding yourself. Jack O'Shea here can get the Elastoplast. You know the green plastic box in the bathroom'?' I nodded. 'Get it.' She went into the kitchen and sat down and my brother saw she had bled on the floor, so *he* starts crying. When I came back she made the two of us wash our hands about six times and dry them very carefully and then we had to pick the glass splinters out of her. At one point she asked very gently if one of us would wipe the blood off her forehead because it was getting in her eye and that made *me* cry all over again. So, of course, that was when my dad walked in. 'The fuck is this?' he wanted to know. 'Guadalcanal?' Neither my brother nor I had the smallest idea what he was talking about and maybe my mother didn't, either, but she said it was nothing to worry about. 'Jack O'Shea here scored a goal through the window. You'd better board it up and ring a glazier.' I started to ask who Jack O'Shea was and my brother started to ask what a glazier was and then my mother yelled at my father not to be picking up bits of glass without work gloves on, that the house couldn't cope with more than one casualty at a time, and told me to get on with picking the glass out of her arm and I said why didn't I have gloves if Dad was supposed to have them and she closed her eyes and shook her head slowly from side to side. I remember my father coming back into the room with a bucket and dustpan

and brush. He stopped and looked at my mother sideways, kind
of, and said, 'Where did it all go wrong, George?' and the two
of them were roaring laughing. Although she must have looked
ridiculous because neither me nor Shane, my brother, had much
experience putting on Elastoplasts. We – we basically did her up
mummy-style. And then my father said maybe it would have been
better if she'd taken off the clothes she was in before we started
and she said 'Feck, why didn't I just step into the shower?' and he
said 'Good point but anyway I put the dress soaking in hot water,'
and my mother said fuck about eighteen times, she never, ever, *ever*
used that word, she'd say shit now and again and feck but never
that one but now she was goin' like a sailor and my father totally
taken aback, looking at her, mystified, and she sort of put her head
back and closed her eyes again. 'How long ago did you put it in the
hot water?' she asked, very quietly, like she was praying. 'Twenty
minutes ago,' my father said. 'Straight from the kettle.' She gave
this long sigh and shrugged. 'Hot water cooks blood on to fabric,'
she told him. 'Bloodstains require the coldest possible water.' I can
still hear her saying it, like a song: 'Bloodstains require the coldest
possible water.'

'So that purple thing is fucked, then?' my father asked, not
bothered much, and she said he wasn't to be swearing in front of
us and he had to sit down, he was laughing so much because of
how she'd been swearing a few minutes earlier. Shane started to
ask what Gudakennel was and neither of them knew what he was
talking about – I think it was maybe ten years before either of us
worked out what my father'd been on about. I learned two things
that day that turned out to be useful.'

Mickey counted them off on his fingers. 'One, that if you want
to get bloodstains out of cloth, you use cold water, not hot. Ma
used to say that she had the most expensive dusters in the world
because you couldn't use the lavender dress for anything other
than dusters after my father cooked the blood into it. Two, that

when you think you've got every sliver of broken glass you're wrong and the best asset you have is the soft side of a bar of soap. Ma went down on her hands and knees with a bar of Palmolive and picked up glass we never knew was there.'

Mickey was smiling at the memory, draped in the chair in total relaxation. He seemed to have a cat-like capacity for complete stillness, matched, based on his reaction to my startle reflex in the airport, by a feline ability to spring into defensive action.

Once his father had inexpertly boarded up the window, he took the two lads outside and played football with them. Looking back, Mickey figured his father was assessing if the window-breaking kick had been a lucky fluke. He never figured out how his father decided that the younger of his offspring had a talent for football – a talent his older brother didn't have. This older brother, Shane, was coordinated like a Lego figure made by a drunk, Mickey said. To this day, couldn't dance. Even at the gym, they would always put him in the back row so he wouldn't put other fitness freaks off their rhythm. Shane was fit. Super fit. Just didn't have it for football, whereas Mickey, at seven, had moves he didn't know he had. Soon he was involved in teams and clubs and training. Medals and trophies followed.

'Kept where?'

'Under the bed,' came the instant response.

'Under whose bed?'

Under the bunk he and Shane shared, Shane on the top bit. Seeing my question, he laughed. It was a small house, so you couldn't be dedicating, like, a coffee table or a special display to yokes you won for sport. Anyway, everybody in the family won prizes at something. Shane was good at photography. Good enough to have survived the cuts at the agency where he now worked. Mairéad won all round her at Irish dancing. She was the middle child. Peter developed apps. And the baby, Lucy, won painting competitions.

'Bunch of over-achievers.'

He was startled by that, as if every family had stocks of varied awards under their bunk beds. He and his siblings each did what they liked outside of school and that was all there was to it. Lucy was coming up to her Leaving Cert and wanted to do graphic design. Peter had just about got a Leaving Cert but had been earning a living from his apps since he was fifteen.

Was he close to his siblings? Again, he seemed surprised by the question.

'Compared to what?' he wanted to know.

'Other families you know?'

They wouldn't be living in each other's pockets, he explained, but they got on great. He looked baffled by the thought that they *mightn't* get on great.

'Parents proud of you?'

'Me or all of us?'

I shrugged.

'I don't think so. I mean, pride doesn't – pride never came into it. Like if you asked me would I be proud of my father, how could I answer that? He's my father? It wasn't ever a project, you know, in our family, just living and doing stuff and – and –'

'And?'

'Laughs. I know it sounds…That's the thing, though, it's always funny when we're around each other. Always laughing. Bit of craic. It's like, God, how do I put this? It's like Ma and Da found us funny and good for a laugh. They weren't pushing – like, they'd be pleased if something went well, if a game went well or Shane had a picture in the paper, that sort of thing, but that was just *work*, d'you know what I mean? Like to this day it wouldn't strike my father to ring up and say congratulations the time it was on the telly me meeting the President, as if that made me better in his eyes. He'd give me an awful slagging, more likely. He's known us all from the beginning, so he wouldn't be deciding you were better or worse, each of us is just the family and – well, you know yourself. I don't mean he wouldn't be pleased when fellas down the pub would be trying to buy him a pint after I'd had a good match but he wouldn't take it and, anyway, all he drinks is shandy and you can't drink that much shandy.'

'How did your mother die?'

'Breast cancer. Seven years ago.'

Silence fell heavily. He examined his hands for a long time before looking at me again. I waited. He waited.

'She died at home,' he said. 'Shane got time off and I postponed my final exams. She wanted everything to go on as normal as long as she could. They wanted to do all these treatments but our local GP basically told her she could get a year and a half of total fucking misery – I'm sorry for the French – or a year that wouldn't be great and she said she'd take the year. Slightly less than a year, she got. It was all right. I remember her saying to me that we'd be grand after she was gone but my father would be useless. He was always useless, she said. Couldn't put a nail in a wall without hitting a water pipe or an electrical cord. And Jesus, she said, don't let him near plumbing. Even that plunger thing for the drains. She'd be laughing when she was saying he was useless, like that was why she married him. They knew each other. They'd never be coming out with the love stuff and I never remember him buying her flowers or anything, not that he was mean, it just wouldn't strike him. They were just parts of the same thing and since she died, he's not bereft or anything, he's like he's waiting for something that's more important than what's going on at any given moment, except maybe at the height of a match, Shane says he's like himself then, his real self like he used to be, the excitement wiping everything else out. He doesn't talk about Ma but he gets a kick out of when we do – me spraying the glass all over her and him ruining the lavender dress by boiling the blood into it, that sort of thing.'

After his mother's death, he had finished his exams and become an actuary. He announced the profession as if he expected a negative reaction. I asked him why.

'Oh, you know the jokes about actuaries being folk who couldn't take the excitement of being accountants.'

'No, hadn't heard them. All I ever heard about actuaries until recently was a tongue-twister I used to administer to broadcasters who tended to skip syllables. The actuary's honorary secretary showed her extraordinary literary superiority by working literally solitarily in the library particularly regularly during February.'

He tried it a couple of times before giving up without much regret and moving on to the urban legend that actuaries were always boring. This surprised me, because the only other actuary I'd known was a managing director who loved adventure and risk so much, Hazard could have been his middle name. The possibility of being seen as professionally boring didn't seem to bother Mickey, probably because 90 per cent of the people who knew of him knew him as a sportsman, rather than as a number cruncher with a healthily remunerative job in a major insurance company. An insurance company that was enamoured enough of being associated with his sporting prowess, they happily allowed him generous time off for training and match play while promoting him steadily up through the ranks. He did a lot of public appearances for them, he agreed, and appeared in their TV ads, but he was also, he affirmed unselfconsciously, very good at the day job, even if he didn't spend as much time on it as did most of his peers. Signs on it, none of them resented him getting promoted or felt that it was just because he was a sporting great, not that he would ever so describe himself.

'How *would* you describe yourself?' I asked.

'Lucky. Easygoing.'

Single, too, although, he claimed, that wouldn't sustain for much longer. He was in a relationship with a nurse named Paula and they planned to get married the following year. In Paris.

With his siblings and father present, together with her brother and parents. They'd have a party when they came home from the honeymoon. They didn't want a big production. Paula was a private person. They probably wouldn't even tell their friends until they came back. Although they wouldn't be that secretive, either of them, so if it got out, what's the problem? Maybe there would be pictures of him in the paper but, sure, that happened all the time.

'Say if one of Paula's friends has a picture of her on their Facebook account and sends that to a paper or Journal.ie or whatever?'

The shoulders went up and the hands went out, palm up: shit happens. The gesture reminded him and he flipped his left wrist to look at his watch. 'We're in injury time,' he said, smiling. 'You get all you needed?'

'Just one more thing before you go. At the end of these two or three sessions, what do you want to have achieved?'

'I'd like to be comfortable with where I'm going with my career.'

'Grand. See you a month from now.'

In the four weeks between appointments, I managed – courtesy of my sports-mad husband – to catch a glimpse on television of Mickey playing a match. I think it was a quarter final of something. On the pitch, he was a different man from the one who sat in our boardroom in his Armani suit and his thin-soled highly polished shoes. As a footballer, he was a mass of contradictions: taller than most of his team, heavy with muscle, yet as fast and flexible in play as a much smaller, lighter man. He also had a driven determination about him that surprised me. It surprised a player on the opposing team, too, and floored him. Towards the end of the match, Mickey was injured but not severely, although the injury was evident next time he turned up in our offices – a cut to his face, healing under a criss-cross of slender steri-strips. He grimaced dismissively when I mentioned it. As long as it wasn't a knee, he said, he was grand. I remembered the man in the airport saying something to Mickey about his knees. He might be easygoing and lucky but he had been injured often enough, down through the years, to have somewhat unreliable knees.

'You said, the last day, you wanted to get comfortable with what you're going to do with your career,' I reminded him. 'Start me with how comfortable you are with where you are, right now, in that regard?'

'Oh, grand.'

'Nothing that's a problem because of you getting leave for coaching here?'

He shook his head.

'So?'

He thought for a long time and then presented a picture, the caption to which might read 'An Embarrassment of Riches'. First of all, in sporting terms, he believed that, absent a major injury, he had a minimum of three, maximum of five, good years left in him. Good years, he stressed. He didn't want to be hanging around after he'd given his best and he didn't want some new manager to have to be brutal with him like – and he mentioned a name of another famous footballer who had been retired against his will and that of the fans a year or so earlier. That was a manager's job, he said, whether a player liked it or not.

'Would you have ambitions to be a manager?'

'Not really.'

'What does that mean?'

Every player, he suggested, at some stage speculates about their own potential, either as coach of a team or as manager. So, at various stages in his own career, he had looked at both possibilities.

'I'd probably be a better coach than I would be a manager,' he murmured. 'I'm good at spotting talent and I'd be all right at encouraging fellas, you know? Like even in our own team, I'd spot something that'd be holding a lad back and be able to show him without him getting pissed at me. I'd be good at that, all right. I'd be all right, like, as a coach. I wouldn't be that good as a manager.'

'Don't managers have financial responsibilities? I'd've thought you'd have those skills?'

'Oh, that'd be no problem,' he said casually. 'The thing is…'

He sat silent for quite a while, considering the issue.

'The thing is, I could *get away* with it, in management. I could. I really could. I get along even with difficult lads. Most of what you have to do, you don't have to get combative about it.'

I suggested he had been pretty combative in the match that had left him injured. He laughed and said that he was a hoor when the blood was up, no doubt about that. But he meant in management terms. An awful lot of the stuff that got into the papers about managers fighting with players was for reasons that had nothing to do with good management.

'How so?'

'If you're managing anything, doesn't have to be sport, could be business equally, it's the routine that's 80 per cent of it. You don't have to be doing wonders or making big statements. You just have to get a routine going so that everybody is – d'you know – so that discipline is just *there*, all the time. Expected. Like a habit, more or less.'

'Character is made in the small moments of a life?'

'Yeah. That's good, that is.'

'I didn't say it. I stole it.'

He made me say it again and asked me where it came from. Some nineteenth-century clergyman, I told him.

'It's true. Footballers should just play football the best they know how and that's what they want to do. Of course, lads are going to break the rules but if the rules are clear and if the team has a bit of pride, they'll usually come back into line. Maybe not if there's an addiction…But, yeah, I could get away with it in management.'

'Get away with what?'

He foosthered around for a while before establishing that he probably had enough expertise, street smarts and personality to be perceived as a good manager, but he lacked the one thing that would make him good in his own eyes, which was a strategic sense. Even now, as a player, he said, it was evident to him that players who mightn't have his instinct or indeed his skill nonetheless had a better grasp of strategy, of the big picture of a game, of where play was going to go, rather than where it was at that moment. One of the better newspaper commentators had touched on it a couple of years earlier and – stung by the criticism – Mickey had focused on strategic issues.

'Then I realised it wasn't a criticism. It was an observation.'

'The difference being?'

'The difference being…well, look at it this way. Let's say you have tests done and the doctor says – oh, I don't know, let's say he says your…your blood count is low or something. It's an observation. You know what I mean? If he said your cholesterol was high and you knew you'd been eating crap, *then* you could take it as a criticism, right? But something that's outside your control, then it isn't a criticism, it's just an observation. When I grasped that, when I acknowledged it, that was great, because I didn't have to be offended or hurt or resent yer man for saying it, it was as… as *impersonal* as if he had said I was left-handed. Not that I am but you know what I mean? Or red-headed.'

What the commentator had noticed, Mickey had realised, was a natural deficit. The footballer, good as he was, didn't have the ability to see the trend of what was happening in the game. Instead, he was always reacting to emerging situations and availing of opportunities as they presented themselves. The fact that he had a natural, physical genius for the game concealed the deficit from most observers and for that he was quietly grateful. But, in his own view, the deficit precluded him from going for a management post, even though his stellar career would predispose clubs and counties to hiring him as a manager. It wasn't a source of regret to him and I asked him why. He looked blank. So blank I felt I had to clarify the query.

'Most footballers would fancy themselves as managers,' I pointed out. 'Well, maybe not most of them but some of them. It's an OK job, right?'

He nodded.

'But you've decided this strategic deficit rules out that option for you?'

'Yeah but that's like you're thinking I've always really wanted that job and I really haven't. Ever. It's just been another possibility.'

'Another possibility?'

'Yeah.'

In the next session, we looked at other possibilities for him when he retired from football. Having (despite my sporting illiteracy) trained sportsmen in Ireland and overseas for employment as TV commentators, it seemed to me that he could do very well in that regard and I was surprised by the vehemence of his rejection of it. Uh, uh, he said. No way, he said. Not a prayer, he said. He would both hate it and be no good at it. He seemed surprised at my surprise and went to some trouble to explain to me that, when it came to football, TV required two kinds of commentators. The first was the impassioned controversialist (although that wasn't how he expressed it – he had a much more interesting, albeit pejorative term). The impassioned controversialists would be men like Joe Brolly or Eamon Dunphy, given to vertical take-off of fury and contempt. Guys who created pitched battles in studio by the venom of their attacks on players or coaches or game plans. Permanently furious fellows who raised the emotional temperature on a programme and pulled in viewers, many of whom knew relatively little about the game itself but who liked the excitement created around it.

'Told you I was easy-going,' Mickey said, laughing. 'I don't even get worked up about my own games, I'm hardly going to be good at getting worked up about someone else's games. Paula once told me I had a shortage of available rage. That was when she was worked up about something her mother had done to her and she wanted me to show solidarity and I really thought I was but it was sort of low-grade solidarity, you know? And that drove her nuts altogether. So I'd be no good at that combative end of commentary.'

But what, I asked him, about the other, non-contentious end of commentary? To do this well, he said, required the understanding of strategy that he didn't have.

'I have it retrospectively,' he said. 'Give me a couple of hours and I'll work out who should have done what and when they should have done it. But you don't have a couple of hours in a TV studio. You have to be able to draw one of them little circles and show how misjudged it was that the so-and-so was in that position at that bit of the game and if I practised from now until forever, I would never be able to do that. I could maybe have done it in print in the past – my writing is OK – but any commentator these days has to be able to tweet clever stuff the minute they see it or do a blog within minutes of the end of the game, not be sitting like a shagging scholar with quill in hand thinking deep thoughts as the dusk draws in.'

He seemed remarkably undaunted by his own wiping away of the possibilities of TV fame and money and I wondered aloud why that was.

'Ah, you wouldn't want to be recognised everywhere.'

'You *are* recognised everywhere. In Cork airport, remember the young lads looking for your autograph?'

'That's different.'

'Is it?'

'That's them recognising someone who *does* something.'

After a minute, he realised that he'd effectively dismissed all TV sports personalities as doing nothing with their lives. He thought about it, then began to laugh.

'I'm sorry but there's no getting around it. Playing football is doing a thing. Being on telly talking about other lads playing football isn't doing anything. It's just sounding off. Like blokes in the pub, except the TV guys get paid for it. Right enough, they may have studied it or – when George Hook goes on about rugby I wouldn't take from him that he was a coach himself but it's still…it's still…oh, I don't know, if I did that I'd be going home afterwards thinking to myself, "What was that about?" I could never convince myself that saying stuff on the television mattered or was important. Plus, there's a lot of sitting around. I'd rather sit around at home. And money isn't – none of us in our house was ever turned on by money. Enough is enough. Enough to get by. I drive a six-year-old car. We have our house. Yeah, I suppose we're in negative equity, the two of us, but I can't see us moving out of that house in the next ten years, so what does negative equity matter? I just – the key thing is that I wouldn't want to be recognised for making smart remarks or even good remarks about what other fellows are doing. It'd be like sucking the life out of my own past and then there's the ones in the pub that'd be coming up spoiling for a fight.'

While he was thinking about what he'd just said, I lobbed an unrelated question at him.

'You happy?'

'Yes?'

'Why d'you say yes like it's a question?'

'I thought you'd be leading somewhere?'

'Most people take time to think about that question.'

He raised his eyebrows, puzzled. Happiness, for him, was evidently a steady state, rather than an anxious aspiration. I let a long silence fall. He drank coffee and waited. This man had no curiosity about his own or anybody else's happiness.

'Have you always been happy?'

'Pretty much, yes. I get pissed when I'm injured and off for a while but mostly I'm happy. Should I not be?'

'Why do you ask that?'

'I was listening to Lyric driving home recently and the one presenting the programme said that unhappiness was a – no, maybe I have it wrong. What she actually was on about was being happy as a child. She didn't get into being happy when you're grown up but she said that having an unhappy childhood was almost a – a – Jeez, I can't remember the word she used…'

'Prerequisite?'

'Yep. Prerequisite for if you were going to be truly creative in your adult life. She said all the composers she was playing that afternoon had the most Godawful unhappy childhoods. I can't remember the examples now but I remember she picked out one exception. Mendelssohn had a happy childhood. He was the only major composer – classical composer – who had been happy as a child. So I thought maybe the same thing applies, that I wouldn't have a great career because I had a happy childhood or that maybe I should be more driven, have higher expectations of myself and goals and stuff and being happy was – well it was really being smug and not getting motivated enough. I don't score high for ambition on those questionnaire things.'

The 'questionnaire things' turned out to be part of a self-assessment process within the insurance multinational for which the footballer worked. Much as you might find in a women's magazine, albeit with psychological support and validation; for each question, six optional answers were supplied. You opted for whatever suited you. Whenever I've done one of those tests, I've generally failed to find a single answer that comes remotely near to where I'm at, but 'none of the above' is not an acceptable response. One of the many great things about being self-employed is that you don't ever have the time to fill in such forms.

Mickey had a pattern, according to the professionals who administered tests within his company, of being on the low side when it came to drive, ambition and determination to get to the tippy top.

'It's not a good finding,' he said thoughtfully. 'If I wasn't a sports star, it would probably tell against me. As it is, they regard it as an anomaly.'

'Tell against you?'

'When it comes to promotion. When it *has* come to promotion, in the past, I suppose I really mean. They mightn't have promoted me so far if I didn't compensate for my lack of drive by serving a marketing function.'

I commented that he didn't seem very bothered by this possibility and he said maybe that was part of his drive deficit. I looked sceptical.

'Why would I be bothered about not getting promotion when — according to these tests — I don't *want* promotion?'

'But do you?'

'Want promotion?'

'Yes.'

'Now or in the past?'

'In the past.'

In the past, he had very much wanted promotion. Entry level money was poor and executives at that level tended to spend most of their time on unrewarding completion and compliance tasks; completing projects largely managed elsewhere in the company or ensuring that every detail of a report met external standards and breached no guidelines. It was, he said, only when an actuary reached his current level that they had autonomy about how to approach their workload and variety in the elements that made up that workload.

'Do you want promotion *now*, then?'

'God, no.'

The answer was as fast and instinctive as the much earlier response to the query about his happiness.

'Why not?'

He had to think about that one. He knew he didn't want it but it took him a while to work out that his reflex had a rationale behind it. Right now, promotion would not appeal to him because it would move him to a level at which he would be less involved in undertaking analyses and more committed to managing the people who did the analytical works.

'The way it is now, I can be totally immersed in a very interesting project,' he said eventually, 'whereas if I get promoted, I would never really have that total immersion ever again – I'd be skating across the surface of other people's work. And doing all the day-to-day management stuff like briefings and assessments and goddam meetings.'

For the first time in several sessions, he leaned forward, not relaxed, looking at the floor as if he suddenly had a problem with the carpet. I knew that sign. He had hit the nub of his own problem. Cue to me to shut up.

'The thing I have to consider,' he said after a moment or two, 'is if my dislike of small things – well, maybe not small things but operational things I could get over, I could learn to tolerate and cope with – if my dislike of those things is just laziness, is avoidant behaviour. Should I take the extra responsibility and work my way into it? Am I just being lazy? I don't mean physically lazy. But maybe intellectually lazy. Maybe a deeper level of commitment? God, I don't know. You see, there's absolutely *nothing* that attracts me to the next level in my company. Nothing wrong with the lead team. Good guys. Genuinely good guys. Most of them really enjoy what they do and it shows. It wouldn't be that boring. But if you asked me would I like the title? No. Not at all. I know who I am. But maybe that's too easy for me to say. Maybe I'm extrapolating from the fact that so many people know me from sport – d'you know? That it's a form of arrogance, not humility, that makes me not needing a better title. Doesn't matter. I just don't need more money or a title or an office on the fifth floor and that leaves me with the fundamental puzzle. Am I letting someone down by not wanting to climb up the corporate ladder? Paula, the last time I asked her, said not to be bothering her with metaphysical oul' shite and I haven't had the courage to go back and get a definition of what constitutes metaphysical oul' shite. Nobody else in my family – I don't owe anybody else in my family anything.'

He ground to a halt, looking defeated by his unavailing search for someone towards whom he could feel an overwhelming sense of duty, which would in turn impel him towards promotion. He began to mutter short non-sequiturs. He was happy doing what he did – was there something wrong with that? He hadn't put it the right way when he'd said he didn't owe his family anything, what he'd meant was that nobody in his family would want anything from him or for him other than what he would want himself. And anyway, it wasn't like the market for what he did was suddenly going to contract.

He seemed to want to interpret his own contentment as an un-acknowledged camouflage for sloth. Everybody but him, he told me, seemed to have a five-year plan for themselves, whereas he didn't even have a one-year plan. For the most part, he just did what was in front of him demanding to get done, took care of the people who clearly needed taking care of and, when he considered tomorrow, warmly expected it to be at least as good as today, if not more so.

'Is your happiness useful?' I asked.

Fecking right it was useful, he told me in a sudden burst of energy. It was useful because in boring times at work, or when other executives were stressed, they'd wander into his office. His office was called Comedy Central, he surprisingly announced.

'It's not that I'm funny myself,' he added hastily. 'I'm not funny.

I just about got away with it the day of Shane's wedding. The guests were in good humour and he made a great speech himself so nobody noticed me that much. Don't get me wrong. I wasn't offensive or anything. I just wasn't that funny and a best man really ought to be funny. I'm just not. It's called Comedy Central, I think, because other people get funny when I'm around. I'm no competition but I'm always up for a laugh. I can get through a lot of work and when I take a break, I find it gives me more energy, so I really welcome visitors, even if they want to bitch or complain or talk about their problems. Why wouldn't they? They don't want to go to someone who's upset themselves. They want to be around someone life is treating right and maybe it will rub off on them a bit.'

I went and got more coffee. When I returned to the room, Mickey was standing up on a ladder someone had left in the corner, examining books on a top shelf. He climbed down without comment and went at the coffee.

'So what do you make of me?' he demanded through a chocolate Kimberley.

'Go back to what you wanted to achieve out of being coached.'

'I suppose, being honest with you now,' he said, as if he'd been lying like a rug on all previous meetings, 'I suppose I wanted confirmation that the way I was thinking was all right. I know, I know,' he said, flagging me down with one of those big punishing hands, 'you haven't confirmed anything. But I've worked it out for myself. I need to stay where I am. Getting a higher-up job isn't – wouldn't be progress for me. And it's not just that I don't want to be promoted to what my da would call my level of incompetence. I could probably develop the competence to perform adequately at the next level but it wouldn't be playing to my strengths.'

Mickey's father hadn't invented the concept of being promoted to your level of incompetence. It's called the Peter Principle, after one of the two writers of an eponymous book. Laurence J. Peter and Raymond Hull's principle was that companies keep promoting talented, high-performing staff until they go a step too far and put them at a level for which they're not able. The problem being that, since companies can no longer reduce employees in their hierarchy without being hit with a constructive dismissal case, what happens is that a preponderance of executives in any large corporation end up sitting at a level where they're not competent to be, with any useful work being done by – as the two writers put it – 'employees who have not yet reached their level of incompetence'.

It happens everywhere. A powerhouse saleswoman will be promoted to the post of sales manager. Bully for her. Except that the skills deployed in her former role are of much less relevance in her new role. A great contributor to a radio magazine programme will be promoted to a presenting job. Rounds of applause all around. Except that the offbeat turbo-charged personality which was so appealing in small doses once a week grates when applied to the presentation of a more frequent, longer slot. A branch manager in a financial institution will be elevated to head office, only to find themselves floored by the scale of the role they are now required to fulfil.

Because upward progress by the talented and hardworking seems right and proper in any organisation, because we programme students to be ambitious and to wish to get to the top, because we measure achievement by rank (witness the constant and justified criticism that women are not sufficiently represented at the upper levels in private corporations and public-sector bodies) it seems counter-intuitive to suggest that it is often better to leave executives at a lower level if they prove to be markedly effective at that lower level.

The only authority figure whose work can be used to support such a policy was a Canadian psychologist named Elliott Jaques, whose extraordinarily difficult books about organisational behaviour develop the concept of 'requisite organisation'. Jaques developed a scientific measurement tool which was used by the US

Army to select generals. He's also credited with having invented the concept of mid-life crisis.

Jaques had a number of theories, any one of which would be too dense to visit here (see the Bibliography for books he wrote). However, he did propose that group dynamics tended to distort organisational outcomes, one of those group dynamics being the deeply-rooted belief that any bright person who worked hard enough could and should be promoted right to the top. While this has continued in its place as received wisdom in management training, Jaques's view was that some employees would never be suited to top management, because (I'm simplifying, here) they could not take the 'helicopter view'. Like Mickey, they were excellent at implementation but incompetent at strategic thinking. Logically, then, they should be left – to revert to Laurence Peter's phraseology – at their level of competence.

Jaques's theories make a lot of sense, once they are translated into plain English. Their lack of currency, however, is largely due to the sense that they amount to a limiting predetermination; in other words that, implemented, they could result in objective scientific tests being applied within the workforce which would arbitrarily limit the upward progress of executives, sticking a snuffer down over the candle of individual aspiration and crushing ambition.

Mickey Donohue is a rarity, in his calmly confident self-analysis and his psychological comfort in the face of staying at his current level within his company. He doesn't confuse progress with achievement and – fortunately for him – is part of a family that seems to be rooted in a 'live and let live' mindset which facilitates each of them in doing what they want and having fun while they do it. Pity we don't have more families like them.

CAREER PITFALL #1: YEARNING TO REACH YOUR LEVEL OF INCOMPETENCE

This can happen because of peer pressure or family pressure or an inchoate urge to prove to yourself that you are making progress and living up to your potential.

Your own happiness may not derive from climbing the hierarchy and failure to do so can leave you bitter and twisted – for no good reason.

Five Tips for You as Your Own Coach

1. Be your own person. Don't structure your career to satisfy others.
2. Have a look at your work life and identify the places, types of situation or days that tend to make you happy. Nobody's continually happy but shaping your career around what genuinely gives you a kick is wiser than shaping it around a nagging sense that you should have a better title and a bigger office.
3. Work out how to turn down a promotion. Remember, most bosses offering promotion expect the offer to meet with gleeful acceptance. Make sure your boss knows that you are thrilled to have been offered the opportunity.
4. Explain to your boss and others why promoting you wouldn't have been a good move for your employer.
5. Once your decision is made and communicated, turn off the doubt button.

2

The Woman with the Snails

Claire wanted to discuss her career with me, she told the person who answered our company phone. Me and only me. It was pointed out to her that The Communications Clinic has several people on staff who are better qualified in career planning than I am but she wanted me and only me. Money was no object. Nor was having to come from Cork.

When she arrived, she was early, anxious, in her mid-thirties and a water-drinker. No coffee. No tea. Not even green tea. None of that filth.

She owned and ran a spa, she told me, and despite the recession, was breaking even. Once her new development kicked in, however, she would move into massive profit by franchising it everywhere. This was a game-changer. A regime-disrupter. She glanced around the room as if she expected a competitor to be hiding behind a screen, ready to steal whatever her innovation was before it could disrupt anything.

'We do a snail facial,' she said in a voice so low I wasn't sure I'd heard her correctly.

'A *what* facial?'

'Snail. Snails secrete this wonderful mucous which has such a great effect on skin. It's healing, it stimulates collagen and – you know how your face feels after a normal facial?'

No, actually, I didn't, not being familiar with facials.

'You wouldn't regularly have facials?'

She couldn't have been more astonished if I'd told her I didn't regularly breathe in and out. 'I've never had a facial. Ever.'

That put her off her stroke. I got the sense that I was not the person she'd expected, if I wasn't a regular facial-user, so I didn't add to her dismay by telling her I'd never had hot stones put on my back, either. I just gave her enough time to recover and produce a folder containing a glossy photograph of a woman with four snails crawling on her face. Or slithering. Or whatever it is that snails do. I looked at it with interest, facial snails being new to me.

'You don't find it off-putting?'

I shook my head.

'Most people shudder at the picture,' she said. 'It gives them the heebie jeebies.'

That's probably because they're not on friendly terms with snails. Gardening has turned into a sterile sport involving acres of pebbles with a few rigid, plant-filled boxes at strategic points throughout, which limits the opportunities for snail-spotting. What self-respecting snail is going to hang around an upmarket modern garden? Not like my huge, beautiful and terribly dated garden, over which I have no rights whatever. My next-door neighbour, Mary Linders, really owns it. I just have visiting rights.

Mary Linders (known as Mother Nature) could make flowers grow on the dark side of the moon. She manages to make them grow in Portrane every year, in the teeth of a north-eastern gale coming straight off the sea, driving rain and sea-foam in front of it. The fact that I couldn't tell a chrysanthemum from a sunflower didn't bother her at all. But when she found out that I wasn't good at distinguishing between flowers and weeds, she gently but forcefully suggested that I leave the plants alone and confine myself to gathering snails and throwing them over the fence on to the patch of waste ground behind where I live. As a result, I am the best snail-gatherer in Ireland. Any spare minute I have, you'll find me going through the flower beds, picking snails big and small off the plants until I have ten or twelve in each hand. Remarkably varied, snails are, in size and style of abode, and once they get over the initial shock of being lifted, they crawl (or slither) around on your palm quite contentedly. If snail mucous is good for the skin, I should by now have the softest, silkiest palms in Ireland.

'No, me and snails get along fine,' I told Claire the spa owner.

I thought of offering to be her supplier but, as it turned out, she had her own supply of a particularly effective face-crawling snail and wanted to pioneer the snail facial in Ireland. The efficacy of a snail facial apparently depends on the snails involved being large and of roughly the same size, because they cover more ground – sorry, skin – than little lads do. The bigger the snail, the bigger its footprint, so to speak.

'My problem is that I don't know the right people,' Claire said. 'I'm not connected. I mean, I network but…'

'How do you network?'

'Well, I go to events and speed-date. In networking terms,' she added hastily.

'How do you mean?'

'You sit down at a table in front of another entrepreneur and they have ninety seconds and you have ninety seconds and then you move on to the next person. The thing is that at the last one I was at, the women I met were very nice but not really a market for my spa, you know what I mean? Like one was an unemployed book-keeper and an other one was running a crèche and there was a hairdresser and a Polish woman named Roma who does cleaning. Office-cleaning, you know? She used to be an accountant back in Poland. There's a lot of Poles where I live. The local Super Valu has a whole display of Polish food and that. Pickles and those biscuit things. It was a great event.'

'Why?'

'Well, it's important for women to network. It's very motivational.'

'Why?'

'How do you mean, why?'

'Why is it motivational to meet someone who does office-cleaning?'

'There's always a great atmosphere. It's very supportive.'

'How is it supportive?'

'Well, you know.'

'No, I don't know.'

'Just,' she said, as if it was obvious how meeting someone who ran a crèche or did book-keeping would keep you going in the face of the slings and arrows life throws at you. I nodded, because it seemed more civil than saying 'Speed-dating with other sole traders in businesses unrelated to your own allows for the brisk exchange of business cards and shag all else.'

'Have you ever got any business out of these networking sessions?'

'Well, I would have given out vouchers entitling people to a discount. But the thing is this. It's really good. It builds up your confidence. They're not the right people, though.'

'The right people for what?'

'I don't move in the right circles.'

'What are the right circles?'

'Like you move in.'

'What circles do I move in?'

Her eyes lit up as she outlined for me my life of glamour and the celebrities with whom I socialise. People like Bressie and Roz Purcell and Aoibhinn and Miriam O'Callaghan. People, she said wistfully, that you see in photographs at premières and receptions.

'Oh,' I said, 'like in *VIP* magazine?'

'Exactly,' she said. 'And Norah Casey and Sinead Desmond and Maura Derrane and Pippa.'

'The girl with the famous behind?'

'*No*. Pippa O'Connor who's married to Brian Ormond. Have you *seen* the pictures of the baby?'

I had to admit that I had not. She didn't say, 'Keep up, would you?' but it was clearly egging to be said. I had a mad urge to raise her a baby picture by mentioning Brian O'Driscoll and Amy Huberman's daughter with the earphones on but didn't think it would advance the situation.

'You're so successful,' she said, 'you'd know those kinds of people. I thought you could put me in touch with them. Like Norah Casey really knows how to make businesses successful.'

'How would meeting Norah Casey solve your snail problem?'

'She could come to Cork and have the facial and then she could be the ambassador.'

Since Norah Casey had, earlier that year, ended her association with an RTÉ afternoon TV show because travelling up and down to Cork had been too time-consuming, I couldn't see her going there for the chance of becoming a brand ambassador for snails. I didn't want to get between Norah and a business opportunity but the former dragon has never struck me as having snails in her career path.

'If you want famous people to validate your service, you have to pay them,' I told her. 'They don't do it just to get a free facial. And each of the people you named has their own brand and would be very protective about the values of that brand. I honestly can't see Amy Huberman allowing a picture of her face covered in slugs to be published.'

'It's not slugs,' Claire said, suddenly very cross. 'It's snails.'

'Sorry.'

'Even you?'

I laughed out loud. Having started high end, with the Miriam O'Callaghans of this world, she was coming downmarket very fast. 'You don't need me. I'm not your market. Which is where we need to do a bit of work. Who *is* your market?'

Girls, eighteen to twenty-eight, she decided. Not that she was excluding outliers like me but the younger age-group, whenever they had money, tended to spend it on trying out new stuff. They were the ones who had tried the fish pedicures when they first came in and they were the best market for her innovative approach to skincare.

'If Pippa tweeted about the snail facial, it would go viral straight away,' she pointed out. 'I just know it would.'

'We'll get to Pippa,' I promised. 'But let's start with your marketing and PR plan. Tell me about them.'

They didn't exist. She didn't even have a business plan. Never mind a business plan for franchising snails, she didn't even have one for her own spa. She had been made redundant when her employer moved to China a couple of years earlier and had sunk the substantial lump sum into the venture. Insofar as she had a business objective at the outset, it was that the spa would pay her a decent salary and when things got busy, support a couple of part-time beauticians. Her accountant brother kept the books and everything was grand until the snails took hold and both of them saw the opportunity for major expansion.

'Describe the expansion you want.'

'Just everywhere.'

'In spas you own?'

'No, in other people's spas. With them paying a fee.'

'For what?'

'For the rights to use my snails. And the training.'

'Training?'

'Each beautician would get – hold on.'

She disappeared into a bag that had joined-up initials on it. Gucci, perhaps? Out came a laminated certificate. It had a seal on it and a gold embossed heading which read 'Mollusca Skincare'. Mollusca Skincare, the flowing script announced, hereby confirmed that Terry Prone had completed the Cochlea Application Course and was qualified to administer it.

'They're the Latin words for snails,' Claire said.

'Very impressive,' I agreed, wondering if she'd leave the sample vellum with me. Latin words and gold leaf might improve my market value. When she put it back in the putative Gucci, I was quite disappointed. Also worried that she might produce it to someone else. I've had enough rumours circulate about me without adding one about credentials in managing rampant snails.

'Of what does the training consist?'

'It's very hands-on.'

'Mmmm?' I murmured, because jamming my lips together stopped me from laughing out loud.

'They have to be taught to apply and reapply the snails to achieve optimal coverage. We supply a light pen to identify – at various stages throughout the procedure – which areas require more attention.'

Another dive produced the light pen. It was a small torch. Nothing more than a small torch. But then, why would you need anything more than a small torch to ascertain the smear level? A good small torch would have no problem revealing the shiny path taken by each snail. The deal seemed to be that the snails were gently removed and replaced to ensure a good overall slime, which I thought might be a bit stressful for the snails but who am I to be judgemental given my merciless track record of removing them in bundles from my garden and sending them to a snail refugee camp over the wall?

Claire, not satisfied that she had sufficiently impressed me with the training afforded as part of the franchise deal, went to great lengths to explain that this training also included a manual of information about snails so the beautician would be able to answer any questions put by their customers. (Understandably, if you're lying on your back for three quarters of an hour with snails traversing your face, you'd want to talk about something and because of your situation, snails might have what the marketing folk call TOMA or 'Top of Mind Association'.)

'And there's a separate workbook about hygiene and caring for the snails,' Claire added.

'And what does the client spa pay for the training and the rights?'

'My brother says it should be fifty K.'

'Based on what?'

'Sorry?'

'Why has he picked that amount?'

She shrugged and said she thought it should be less, because if *she* had to pay out that much, her own spa would go under but the brother was convinced that longer-established spas would be doing better than hers was and might, into the bargain, benefit from having something brand new to offer.

'How many spas do you plan to sell to?'

'Nearly all of them. Well, if I could get someone to front for it, like – '

I had to interrupt her before Pippa got another outing.

'Whoa. How many are there *in toto*?'

'I wouldn't know.'

'You should. You're going to have to. How can you work out how much you will earn if you don't know the size of your potential market?'

The putative Gucci got another go. This time, the light pen AKA torch went back in beside the certificate qualifying me in snail application and out came a pad and pen.

'You need to establish how many spas operate in Ireland,' I suggested. 'You also need to find out how the franchise works elsewhere, because I assume the snail idea didn't start in Ireland, and find out what their hit rate is – in other words, what percentage of the spas approached by the snail supplier actually picked up the franchise.'

Claire made notes but sighed while so doing. Her comfort zone was defined by Amy, Brian and Pippa. Outside that, the going got rough. Although what had begun to worry me, on her behalf, was the question of what defined her *brother's* comfort zone.

'What does your brother think you could make in any one year from the snails?'

'He hasn't really said. He's in Australia.'

'Now?'

'Since last year. But he still does the books. He's having a great time out there. He's my little brother. He's only twenty-four.'

Aha, I thought. This explains why the brother is not all over the business plan. He's all over the kangaroos and the beer and the blondes on Bondi Beach. He's telling his big sister not to worry, it'll all be grand. He's paying not a blind bit of attention to her and her snails.

I started to go, step by rudimentary step, through all the numbers Claire needed before she could even *begin* to think of the snail enterprise. It looked as if Pippa and company were safe from her for a long time to come. When she got to the tenth page, she put down the pen and wagged an evidently sore hand loosely from the wrist. I offered coffee. Suddenly, coffee held enormous appeal. I pointed out the ladies' room. When we regrouped, a different Claire was in action. A grimmer, much more realistic Claire.

'I don't know how I'm going to be able to do all this,' she said reproachfully, as if I had asked her to collect ten sacks of smoke-free coal and deliver them to me each day. By hand. 'I mean, all this research. How am I going to find the time to do it? It'll take forever. I don't know where to start.'

She tore the pages – by now about twenty of them – out of the notebook and began to group them. It took her about ten silent minutes to reduce the scatter to eight small piles and while she did it, she forgot I existed. Then she went back and put some of the clusters together so she ended up with four, three of them fat, one of them consisting of only a single sheet.

Then she took one pile and made notes from it on to two fresh pages, scrunching up the originals and binning them. Eventually, she turned the pages around and took me through what they stood for.

The first action was market research. She had to find out how many spas or beauty salons that provided more than hairdressing or manicures existed in Ireland. Then she had to work out how to market to them, since, as she somewhat bitterly acknowledged, simply getting a celeb to submit to snailing would not be enough. She got briefly distracted at this point by remembering she had forgotten to put Amanda Brunker on the potential snail-spokesperson list. She added Amanda at the bottom before going back to set-up issues. She understood, she announced, that she would have to get her brother to look at the spa market and work out a likely hit rate. Then, based on how many of them she could tie down, get him to work out how much each would be required to pay for the franchise.

The second bit of paper was on its own and had a sketchy schedule for the various activities she would have to undertake.

The third – comprising two sheets – held nothing but questions:

How do I find out more about franchising?

Say if someone else gets the same idea?

Could someone in a university do a study or something?

Are there health and safety rules? (HIV virus/fish?)

How would I get a logo and should it be different from my own spa business?

Does An Post deliver live things?

Allergies?

Would I be better being the Irish arm of the companies doing this overseas?

Could I be doing with a lawyer?

Storage?

Say if they started OK but stopped paying?

Would I be like HIQA inspecting crèches and how much time would that take or would I need someone else to do it and if so what would be the cost and the cost of running this person's car?

Maybe a pilot? Just one spa?

Put a logo on the light pen?

How big a budget for celebrity endorsements?

The last page seemed to have derived from some of the questions. It included plans to talk to Enterprise Ireland (which seemed sensible, even if I didn't honestly think the state body was going to fall over itself with eagerness to support a snail-based endeavour), *Dragons' Den* (which seemed adventurous, if a tad previous), a potential partner or partners, her bank and some of her existing customers.

'You're not quite sucking diesel,' I said encouragingly, 'but, realistically, you're a lot closer to sucking diesel than when you came in here this morning.'

'Well, I did most of it myself.'

'True.'

'I'm sorry, I didn't mean it like that. I suppose I thought you'd give me the answers.'

'I don't even understand all your questions,' I confessed. 'What's the thing about the fish getting HIV?'

'It's not the fish, it's the water. You know where you put your feet in the water and the fish nibble the corns off your feet? There was something on the web about it being not that safe that the virus could – I don't know – float around in the water, maybe? I can't remember but I'll find it. I need a lawyer, don't I?'

I nodded and suggested that Enterprise Ireland might be able to point her in the direction of a lawyer who would know about franchises and intellectual copyright. I wasn't sure if intellectual copyright applied to snails but she definitely needed someone who could work out a way to give her inalienable rights to the mollusc skincare concept, about which I was becoming ridiculously enthusiastic. I had to stop myself suggesting she research the possible effects of snails on scars, because although some products are available from pharmacies to reduce the appearance of scars, none of them is perfect.

The mood in the room had utterly changed from wide-eyed optimism to a tired but grimly resolute determination. An hour later, Claire's notebook contained a six-month personal action plan. Towards the end, that plan took a skeletal look at public relations. It might be possible, I suggested, to get one of TV3's Xposé girls to get snailed on screen. At around the same time, if her research and her finances justified it, she could look at offering Pippa or Amanda a few bob to go through the procedure and tweet about it afterwards. I could have pointed her at seed capital companies but I figured most of them would not fully grasp the potential of facial snails, so the chances of her amassing capital at the outset were small.

She went off to the bathroom, putative Gucci in hand and came back with make-up refreshed and attitude likewise.

'I know what you were *really* doing,' she announced. 'You were telling me to stop faffing around and just do it. And I will. No offence but you're right, you're not my market so it doesn't bother me you think it won't work. I can promise you that six months from now, I'll be back to you to set up the meeting with Pippa.'

'If you do everything on your action plan, you won't need me for that. You'll have worked out how to reach her yourself.'

'This is exactly what I needed,' Claire said as she left. 'Meeting you is like the first step. I knew I wasn't moving in the right circles, that I didn't know the right people.'

And off she went, happy out, a spring in her step, to go lay snails on faces countrywide. She was right, in one sense. She was going away with what she needed: a rudimentary business plan, an outline marketing plan and a sampler PR plan but she was still – wrongly – convinced that knowing famous people was the key to her future. To that extent, I had utterly failed her. I had given her good value but hadn't divested her of the myth she arrived with.

One of the most deadly business myths is: 'It's not *what* you know, it's *who* you know.' According to this myth, if you're not on first-name terms with the rich and powerful, you will not only not get into the VIP section of any night club, you will, in career terms, never get anywhere. You're done before you start.

I've never come across this myth in other countries. When I've trained executives in the United States or in Britain, they may and do produce all sorts of reasons to excuse themselves for future failure but they don't suggest that they won't get anywhere because they're not sufficiently connected with the powerful. In fact, America has always prided itself on believing the reverse; that anybody from any log cabin in the back of beyond can, for example, get to be president, even if they have no connections other than those they make for themselves. In Britain, it's sometimes said that elites of various kinds can exclude those who don't quite belong, but someone will always point out that if a grocer's daughter could become prime minister, anybody can succeed if they just put their mind to it.

What's interesting about the English elites is how their noisiness is now in inverse proportion to their effectiveness. In the past, they were relatively silent but infinitely effective, when it came to excluding those who did not belong. Nancy Mitford, who came from a family of aristocracy and eccentricity (one of her sisters married the leader of the British Fascists and another fell hopelessly in love with Hitler) wrote a book about the 'tells' that distinguished the gently-born from the rest, pointing out that someone who, greeting a newly introduced stranger for the first time, said 'Pleased to meet you,' was immediately dismissable, since the correct phrase is 'How do you do?'

Back in Mitford's time, a lid-lowered glance between members of the elite was enough to establish 'You and I both know this individual is non-U, so we will go to some lengths to make them feel briefly at home and then ensure that they never visit us again.'

More recently, a lowered-lid glance has not sufficed, so we hear that people near the British royal family, disapproving of Kate Middleton's mother's career as what was then called an air hostess, referred to her among themselves as 'Doors to manual,' an inside joke of crude cruelty. Similarly, her daughter was mocked as 'Waity Katy' because she was prepared to hang around until her prince was ready to ask her to marry him.

The sneering undoubtedly reached Kate Middleton and her mother, just as global appreciation of her rear view reached Pippa Middleton, post-wedding. But the point to be remembered is that the wedding did go ahead, despite the *noblesse disoblige* courtier types. Kate Middleton was not born knowing the right people. Anyone looking at her situation when she was, say, ten years of age would not have bet on her as the future Queen of England. Fortunately for her, the Duchess of Cambridge doesn't seem to have wasted much time disqualifying herself based on not knowing the right people.

The 'It's not what you know, it's who you know' myth seems to be as unkillable as a cockroach in Ireland. Claire is not the only client with whom I have worked who suffered from its time-wasting effects. In her case she was focused on not knowing famous people, celebs. Many other clients were focused on the fact that they came from the wrong place, had gone to the wrong schools or did not know any powerful, influential or rich people.

Some of the strength of this myth may be rooted in our history. Being ruled by another country and being discriminated against because of your native language or your religious belief may have give rise to generationally repeated rebellions but it also, inevitably, taught Irish people the belief that power and influence resided within an impenetrable circle. Belonging outside that circle would limit your education, your freedoms and entitlements and the path your life took, so it cannot be a coincidence that present-day Irish people, or at least some of them, despite the advantages of education, still believe that success resides within a particular golden circle where secrets are shared, deals are done and the sons and daughters of members of the circle stand a better chance of a stellar career than do young people with no such advantage.

Like all crippling myths, this one has a grain of truth in it. Friends tend to do favours for friends and for the children of friends. Of course they do. More than 90 per cent of people who win the lottery do likewise, which is why, when a rich person takes to the streets handing €100 bills out to perfect strangers, it makes headlines. We sit up and take envious notice because most people minded to do others a favour tend to start with those they know and like.

My beautician, Claire, didn't – at the outset of her enterprise – need someone famous to stand by her snails. Perhaps when she had put together a plan for franchising, a method of identifying beauticians – sorry, aestheticians – who might be ready to branch out into snails, tied them down with a solid contract and worked out how to distribute the little lads, she might at that point contact someone reasonably famous who would not charge her a fortune to endorse the new facial. But not at this point in the development of her project. Spending time, at this stage, wondering about sliming the faces of the famous was a waste of her time, as was grieving over her lack of contact with household names. It's a bit like the old story of the drunk who drops his keys and goes looking for them under a lamp post.

'But you dropped them over there,' one of his friends points out, gesturing.

'I know but the light is better here,' responds the drunk.

Looking under the wrong lamp post is a recurring pattern that slows down or permanently halts many a career. Success comes when you start looking in the right place.

CAREER PITFALL #2: LOOKING UNDER
THE WRONG LAMP POST

This happens when you distract yourself from your career focus.

Claire's not the only entrepreneur distracting herself from what her business needs her to do by yearning to be with famous people. Lots of writers take the same route. They believe that if they can get to meet a bestselling author, that author will adopt them and turn *them* into a bestseller, too. Why would they? Why would anybody in their right mind set up someone who might, down the line, represent killer competition?

It's the same with some networkers as well as some seminar and conference-goers. They find one of the speakers enthralling. Not only is that speaker successful at what they do but he's motivational, funny, realistic, exciting and hasn't lost the run of himself. Well, bully for him. The problem arises when a seminar or conference participant becomes convinced that success will follow just sitting down with that speaker. Any good motivational speaker will confirm that they could make a financial killing by hiring a room and agreeing to meet attendees at seminars or conferences for top dollar directly afterwards, because when hero-worship kicks in, it disinhibits its owner's grasp on their debit card. Don't let that happen to you. Most of the insights and guidance you need in your career or your business are available to you from your boss, your colleagues, your mother, Enterprise Ireland or Google.

Hearing them from a well-known or charismatic talker won't make them any more valuable but it could make them a hell of a lot more costly.

Five Tips for You as Your Own Coach

1. Hero-worship your customer, not some charmer off the box.
2. Interrogate the wisdom that's all around you for free.
3. Don't believe famous equals interesting. Except in short bursts, for the most part, it doesn't.
4. When you're at a seminar, speech or conference, make notes and see to what career use you can put those notes. What matters is content, not the warmth of a speaker's personality.
5. Concentrate on making yourself famous, not on tapping into the fame of others.

3

The Couple Crushed
by a Falling Tiger

I was at a meeting in Ernst & Young, who have the poshest offices
in the world in Dublin's Earlsfort Terrace. The meeting was about
their award of Entrepreneur of the Year to the inventor of the
Moo Monitor. You haven't heard of it? Just shows you're not in
agribusiness. Great yoke dreamed up by one of my clients, Dr
Edmond Harty, who heads up a company named Dairymaster in
Causeway, County Kerry. The Moo Monitor tells the farmer when
the cow would fancy a visit from the bull, which saves everybody
(including the cow) a lot of money and the frustration of guessing.

When the meeting is over, I go down the steps into the drizzle
and check my BlackBerry for messages, aware that a man sharing
the drizzle experience, because he, like me, doesn't have an
umbrella, is doing much the same. I'm on one corner of the road,
he's across the way. Each of us looking at our reflections in office
windows as we finish phone calls. Then we're stranded in the cold,
waiting for lifts. We do the 'such is life' shrug at each other and to
my surprise it jump-starts him into walking across to me.

'You won't remember me,' he says.

It has to be like facing over the edge of the Grand Canyon,
that one. You can say of course you remember him and then
prove yourself a liar, or you can say sorry you don't remember
him and insult him straight up. I went for the straight-up insult
and disavowed knowledge – or at least recollection – of him. He
promptly came through with the killer response.

'Well, I sure as hell remember *you*,' he said, shaking his head.

If I'd been more rackety in my youth, this would have scared me. I have friends whose past exploits don't bear discussion. In some cases, they took the form of cartwheeling down the main street of their town as dawn broke after a long alcohol-fuelled night. In others, they ingested mixed substances calculated to mood-elevate them straight to the top floor and leave them locked there.

Sadly, I have no exciting past, no shocking secrets from a misspent youth. Which was why I couldn't figure why this man would remember me with such fervour.

'You gave me great advice,' he said. 'You told me to engage my brain before I engaged my mouth. Best thing that ever happened to me.'

Now, usually, when someone tells me I said something to them on a course that has lived with them ever since, I get a bit wary. Firstly, because they may have mixed me up with some other trainer or public speaker with whom I passionately disagree, but also for fear that I might have been having an off day, back then, and warped the poor man's life on him, even if he doesn't see it as having been warped.

Somewhere a natural law exists which holds that course participants and many of those who attend coaching sessions do not believe they've received full value if they haven't effectively been taken warmly by the throat and given a good talking-to. Negative observations seem to have much deeper impact – which is discouraging – and also tend to be recalled, often with inappropriate reverence, decades later. Guys exist who will maintain to their dying day that getting flogged by a Christian Brother, beaten up by their older brother or chewed out of it by their first boss are the best things that ever happened to them. You can't say 'You're a blighted sorry masochist' to someone for whom such events are the highlight of their lives. Up against that kind of experience, me telling a man to shut up until his brain had clicked in didn't seem too bad.

He had obeyed the instruction, he told me, and it had got him a reputation as being thoughtful, which in the legal firm where he worked was an advantage. Up to the point, five years ago, when the firm had collapsed in the face of the recession. He had another job, he reassured me, albeit at half what he'd been earning back then. I didn't know whether to congratulate or commiserate and while I was dithering between the two, he asked if there was any chance he and his wife could see me at my office? I said sure, we set a time, my taxi arrived and we parted.

His wife, Jasmine, turned out to be a glamorous mother of two. That sounds as if she was a criminal. Headlines always say 'Father of five killed gang member' or 'Mother of three admits larceny.' What their parenthood has to do with their crime beats me. Notwithstanding which, this woman, despite having no criminal record, was definitely a mother of two. Also an accountant with a doctorate in something commercial, a winner of national awards when in academia and used to bonuses which, one year, reached €150K. We're not talking about muck, here. Her salary, when she was on the receiving end of such bonuses, was tipping a quarter of a million a year.

Jasmine's problem, as she sat with her husband in our offices, was that she was about to lose her job. This was in the spring of 2013 and a couple of weeks earlier, it had been announced that IBRC, the entity into which the collapsed Anglo-Irish bank had been folded, was, in turn, for abolition. Later that year, it would be nothing but an acronym nobody quite remembered, except for the Matt Coopers and Arthur Beesleys of this world, they being the guys who write books to remind us, lest we could ever forget, just how badly we were goosed, nationally, corporately and individually, by the collapse of Ireland's banking system.

Come July, Jasmine said, she would have a statutory severance package of about €10,000 and – as she saw it – zero chances of getting another job. Why? Because, God love her, she worked for IBRC and, by inference, had worked for Anglo. Not, she told me, that she ever tells anybody the truth about where she works. Not since the two of them, at his sister's wedding, ended up leaving early because guests turned on her when it emerged she was a long-term Anglo employee. She hadn't tried to get out of IBRC earlier because, back in the day when the two of them were earning hand over fist, they had been sensible. They'd bought a new house – not a pillared mansion but expensive, anyway, and held on, for investment purposes, to their old house. They'd put money in bank shares and because they were clever and provident, had spread them over a number of banks. Then he'd lost his job and been unemployed for a year, which was a major setback. They did console themselves with the thought that, once the state took over Anglo, Jasmine would essentially be a civil servant and could not, as a result, be fired.

Wrong, wrong, wrong. She could. Her termination would be just the latest in a string of circumstances that had put the two of them in debt for more than a million, owning a house worth half its purchase price and technically owning another house in much the same condition.

Niall was currently earning a third of what Jasmine was earning but, come the long, hot summer of 2013 (not that any of us had a clue, at that stage, that it was going to be so warm it improved the very sound of the word 'staycation'), his wife would be on the dole, receiving a quarter of what he was then on. What they were facing, financially, was debt by a thousand cuts, with their two hands tied behind them and the word 'options' applying to anyone but them. They felt like the dogs in the experiment to test resilience, where the animals were thrown in a pool and every time they came up for air, shoved under again. Every time this couple thought they had hit rock bottom, some other charge – like the household charge – came along and pushed them under water. Again. The end result was that the dogs developed what was called 'learned helpessness'. Their natural fight was leached out of them over time. Relentless recurring defeat robbed them of the will to fight, indeed of the will to live. The couple sitting in front of me were not quite at that point but it wasn't far away.

'I want to find and belt whoever dreamed up that ad with the gobshite going around his house sticking up environmentally-friendly light bulbs to save money,' Niall said bitterly. 'It's like it's jeering us – other people can manage in these times by switching light bulbs. Really?'

Their situation will be familiar to many, which is no consolation to anybody. The fact that each job loser has company doesn't help. That old saw that 'misery loves company' isn't true, when it comes to standing in the wreckage of your life and your dreams. This couple, having analysed their finances up, down and sideways, were appalled to find how little they could contribute to their own survival and how much was outside their control. All the significant outgoings in any given month – mortgage, insurance (including health insurance), utilities – were outside their control and represented more than 80 per cent of their budget. Setting out to reduce the 20 per cent still under their control had a flavour of moving the deck chairs around on the *Titanic*.

For a few weeks, at the weekend, they journeyed from Tesco to Lidl to Aldi, buying only half-price special offers in each. They gave that up because it took time and petrol and depressed him by forcing him – in Lidl – to look at drills, sanders and power washers he would have bought, back in the old days of the impulse purchase.

Eventually, they settled on buying online from Tesco, whose site apparently has a function that reminds them of their regular purchases and allows them to compare what they spend one week with what they spent the previous week. The method eliminates the admittedly remote possibility of impulse buying and they've found the level of control they have gained outweighs the transient pleasure once afforded by picking up a personal treat or a gift for another family member. A beneficial spin-off is the reduction of 'pester power' on the part of their children.

They have come to dread the unexpected. Even the ostensibly happy unexpected, Jasmine said, like the birthday of a friend of their twins. 'Try explaining to two five-year-olds that they can't go to a birthday party because we can't afford a present.'

They have pared back their living expenses so far that the only 'treat' they could recall was going to a film six weeks earlier. Their parents are apologetic about not being able to help them, because all *their* savings were in bank shares, too, so they're under pressure as well. Because she's a financial adviser, she came up with a detailed plan to present to the bank to try to get on top of their debt. It was met by silence for six weeks, after which the bank responded with a one-sentence refusal.

Some IBRC friends, they told me, planned to lobby politicians to make them see that IBRC/Anglo staff were being treated unfairly. What they wanted to know from me was this: would the lobbying work? I couldn't come up with a better answer than silence. It wouldn't, would it? they asked. Even opposition politicians wouldn't fight for them, would they?

'We're just not acceptable victims,' Jasmine said, beginning to cry, in that furious way characteristic of a woman who believes crying in public is shameful.

She'd never done anything improper or unethical in her life, never mind in her job. Never given anything but the best advice. But her definition of the unacceptable victim summed it all up. The Anglo people are not acceptable victims. Post-meltdown Ireland rations its sympathies and feeds most of its fuel into the retributive machine, which grinds exceeding small. Having once been riding high, earning big is enough to prove them deserving of righteous contempt. That profane old philosophical T-shirt statement, 'Shit happens,' no longer works: someone's to blame for everything and front and centre are the Anglo guys, personified by this couple. (Although he never worked for Anglo, his job disappeared as a result of what Anglo and other banks did.)

Niall and Jasmine were young, educated, hardworking. With the world at their feet – except the world was in bits. Not that age was relevant; in the last two years, I have encountered and worked with much older people in the same ghastly situation.

Popular coverage tends to assume that older people have suffered much less from the meltdown than younger people. They have their mortgage paid off, goes this thinking, their offspring educated, and they didn't – during the boom – invest in unseen and undeveloped shopping malls in Poland.

In fact, older and ostensibly well-off people have been caught in the wringer, too. Just as real as that of Niall and Jasmine is the plight of, say, hospital consultants who had managed their money to ensure comfortable retirement at sixty or sixty-five and who now face the prospect of working until they are seventy, if they can safely continue to do so.

The couple in our offices, in theory, should have been better able to cope with what had hit them than would older people similarly impoverished. Except that they'd both been hit at the same time, they had young children and they lacked the stress-inoculation protection they might have had if they were old enough to have had a vivid memory of a previous recession. Even if they had such experience, one factor, new in this recession, is the level of blame attaching to all bankers but particularly those who worked in Anglo, who, with some justification, believe that guilt-by-association with the macho men heard in recorded conversations may cripple their chances of another job in financial services.

The arrival of those recordings into the public domain was,

according to my colleague Eoghan McDermott, a deadly blow to many former Anglo executives.

'Some of them had begun to hope that the IBRC period, intervening between the Anglo days and the present, might create a buffer, preventing their career from crashing straight into the Anglo wall,' Eoghan wrote in *The Irish Times* shortly after the tapes were published. 'They had begun to hope that, with Sean FitzPatrick charged and having to pitch up at a Garda station each week to prove his presence in Ireland, prospective employers would pay less attention to the personnel and culture of their previous employer.'

In fact, as Eoghan wrote, one ex-Anglo employee who had a second job interview directly after the publication of the tapes, for which he was so perfectly qualified that his appointment, post-interview, had seemed inevitable, realised the moment he walked into the financial institution's boardroom and sat down facing three top managers in the institution that he was a goner. It wasn't that the members of the interviewing panel were contemptuous. On the contrary, they were polite, considerate and kind. It was obvious, nonetheless, that they were merely going through the motions. They never asked him about the Anglo tapes and he could hardly bring them up and say 'Look, the rest of us weren't like that.'

The couple in my office were beaten down by those realities, crushed by circumstances beyond their control, frightened by a no-option future stretching ahead of them. I suggested that the old rule about eating an elephant applied to them: that anybody can eat an elephant as long as they slice it thinly enough. Slicing their elephant into usable slices, I suggested, started with them having our careers experts look at their CVs to find ways to acknowledge their Anglo history without sinking their interview prospects.

'But before we see either of you again,' I said, 'I need you to do a little research into yourselves. Make a note on your phone whenever you get a thought about Anglo, debt, job prospects or any of that bad stuff. When and where it happens, what triggers it. OK?'

Sure, they said. She remarked that they mightn't have time to eat, sleep or play with their children, because such negative thoughts were so constant in their lives. Fine, I said, just do it and when you're ready for your next session, give me a ring. Interestingly, when the phone call came, a couple of weeks later, it came from Jasmine alone. She thought it might be good if she came on her own. So an appointment was set up and in she came, clutching a printout of when what she called bad Anglo thoughts had hit her, over the previous fortnight.

'It's not accurate in the beginning,' she said by way of introduction. 'I mean, it's accurate about the days but it was only in the second week that I started to record what happened at night. I had to get a small light so I wouldn't be waking Niall up. Will I start with the daytimes? OK. On the Monday, half-way through the morning, one of my colleagues started to play the Anglo tapes on his computer. He had his earphones on but at one stage he stood up without thinking and pulled out the bit that fits in to the computer, you know? And so we all got a blast of one of the worst bits. He was very apologetic but of course someone asked him why the hell he was annoying himself with it and – well, it was just unpleasant. I didn't get involved. I wanted to be anywhere else but I couldn't leave my desk. I was nauseous. Sorry. Nauseated. Not vaguely – it was like the very first time I smoked a cigarette, d'you know when you're so nauseated, it's almost physically painful? Like that. Terrified I was going to throw up in front of everybody. But I was certain that if I stood up, I *would* vomit, so all I could do was sit there.'

Sweat pooling in the semi-circles below her eyes, she sat transfixed, her heartbeat drumming in her ears, looking at her computer screen as if she was studying the data thereon, mouth closed, breathing as deeply as she dared through her nose. The tiff about the tapes died down but her heart continued to pound so that, as the nausea lessened, she began to wonder if she might have a cardiac arrest.

'I thought it might be arrhythmia and the only thought in my head was that probably I was the only person who knew how to use the defibrillator. Fat lot of good it was going to be to me if nobody else could work it.'

Eventually, she got up and went to the bathroom, where she first vomited, then sat on the toilet for a long time 'like a ridiculous version of Rodin's *Thinker*, stinking and shaking and crying.' After ten minutes, she cleaned her teeth, drank a great deal of water and used a perfumed towelette on the back of her neck and under her arms.

Make-up repaired, she went back to her desk. Nobody seemed to have noticed either her distress or her absence but then, she observed, the five currently sharing an office once occupied by four times their number weren't actually friends in any real sense. They were survivors, thrown together by circumstance, each trying to get out of IBRC before it formally got rid of them. Their priorities were personal, not communal. She noted all this in her diary without sympathy. They might share an experience but it had not welded them into a collective, had not glued them into a mutually-concerned community. Interesting, this. When a company downsizes, the reverse usually happens. Morale tends to rise as those who are left create a new sense of 'us'.

'Back in the day, we'd have hardly known each other's names, we were so busy in our different areas,' Jasmine said. 'If I'm to be very honest? Now that we've moved into desks that are closer to one another, I don't *want* to get to know them. It made sense not to have five people scattered over a big space but I'm sorry we moved closer together, I'd actually prefer it the other way. But anyway, I didn't want any of them knowing I – knowing that there was something wrong with me. None of their beeswax. I know that sounds horrible but they're not real to me and I don't want them to get real.'

She rubbed her hands over her face and started to go back to her diary notes, then stopped and looked unseeingly around the room.

'It's not just them. That aren't real to me, I mean. I have this sensation all the time that I'm – I'm at a distance from everything. Like I'm witnessing my own life from a distance. Or acting me in situations that are familiar – with the children and so forth – but acting me very badly and not caring that much. My five-year-old did that thing the other day; waving his hand in front of my face and going, "Earth to Mammy," and even as I responded, I wasn't totally *there*, even though I felt guilty and was trying to convince him I was paying full attention.'

Jasmine's attention to detail, in her diary-keeping, was impressive. It wasn't just that she was concentrating on a task. It was as if the task was more interesting, or perhaps more productive in some inchoate way, than the rest of her current life. She talked of her own dismay, by the third day, at realising how much of her mental time was involuntarily taken up by the meltdown. Whether she was analysing data, shopping, cooking or picking up the children, she would frequently find herself concentrating on some aspect of or event during the collapse of the bank. It might be a phone call that she had received more than a year earlier from a friend working in another bank, quietly suggesting Jasmine get the hell out of Anglo because the friend was hearing rumours to the effect that it was all going to end in tears. It might be the first time she and Niall sat in a pub with colleagues and shared whatever information they had, realising in the process that their dream jobs had turned into nightmare jobs. It might be an almost physical replay of the bizarre interview Sean Fitzpatrick gave to Marian

Finucane when the bank was already half-way down the tubes, in the course of which he had opined that Ireland was spending way too much on social welfare payments. Or – more often than not – it might be the meeting at the bank where Niall and Jasmine had their mortgage, at which a banker who was much younger than either of them lectured them about the need to stop shopping in Tesco and go to Lidl or Aldi instead.

I asked her to describe these memories. They were, she said, of a transient vividness so pronounced that they seemed more real than reality. For a few moments, when they happened, she wasn't recalling an event the way she might recall a normal meeting, conversation or argument. She was *back* in the situation as it played out, experiencing precisely the same emotions that hit her during the original experience. It was, she pointed out, one of those memories she had been reliving when her little boy had done his 'earth to Mammy' intervention. Keeping a journal over the past fortnight had made her realise how falsely immediate each memory seemed and that, while this might be the first time she'd noted down what was going on in her head, she had no doubt whatever that the same process had been repeating itself for weeks and months. That very repetition should have lessened her sensitivity to each recurrence but that desensitisation didn't seem to be happening.

'To be honest, it's as if I'm *more* involved, more shocked, more sensitive each time,' she said.

Having taken me through the first week of day-time episodes, she moved to night times, which were part of the record from the middle of that initial week. The journal recorded terrifying nightmares in which her parents, her children and herself were victims of catastrophic but imprecise events in some way linked to what had happened to the bank.

'It was Niall who said I should include it, because every other night he was hearing me crying in my sleep and waking me up. The only time I don't have nightmares now is when I take a Stilnoct. And before you ask me how often, I ration them.'

'How often?'

'Three a week. I get desperate for sleep. That's the other thing. I forgot to say to you, if Niall and I ever get divorced, it will be because he was able to sleep like the dead throughout all this. It drives me out of my mind. We go to bed and we're talking about money because that's all we ever talk about these days and I say something, maybe about an aspect of our finances that I'm really up to ninety about, and I get no answer from Niall and I listen and the breathing gives him away, he's fast asleep. And then he snores, so I'm lying beside him doing mad sums in my head, like 'I'll turn the other way when he's snored twenty-five times and then for sure, he'll do that snorting thing and throw my count off so I have to start again and then I *really* think I'm going crazy. Because I have to look and sound and behave professionally at work the next day, I may decide after four hours of complete insomnia that I absolutely have to have some sleep and I slide out of the bed and go get the sleeping pill I should've taken when I was going to bed and, OK, it knocks me out but because I've taken it late in the night, it leaves me hung over in the morning so I'm dragging myself around like someone hit me with a two-by-four until nearly lunchtime.'

She talks about a gym membership for twenty-four months given to her by her parents as a Christmas gift just a year before and how she keeps meaning to go back to do workouts but never getting around to it and anyway, they can no longer pay child-minders, so have less available time for fitness.

'The nightmares are bad and it's wonderful to have a night's sleep that is just – poof, gone, like a fire blanket being lowered over me, but when I wake up the following morning, when I realise, "No more sleep, no more warm dark oblivion, now it all starts all over again" – that's the worst of all. At that point, I would give anything just to go back to sleep, to not wake up. To never wake up. That would be the best. To never wake up. And no, I'm not awash in suicide ideation. If not wanting to relinquish the solace of sleep were a definition of suicidality, every teenage boy would qualify.'

I asked her to leave me the hard copy of her journal and allow two weeks before she saw me again. If she needed help preparing for a job interview, I'd get someone other than me to do it. What *I* wanted her to do was a little research.

'Into what?'

'Post Traumatic Stress Disorder.'

She bridled and demanded to know if I thought she was mentally ill. I said mildly that I wasn't competent to judge. I wanted her to learn a bit about PTSD and on her next visit discuss with me whether or not *she* believed she was a sufferer. Because if she was, there was no point in wasting time with me; she would need to spend time with an expert in that disorder.

She left in great dignity and high dudgeon and we heard nothing from her for three weeks. Then she made an appointment and early one morning, appeared with notes about PTSD.

'I can see why someone might misinterpret some of what I've been experiencing as PTSD,' she said with conspicuous restraint.

'Someone like me?'

'Yes.'

'In other words, me?'

'Yes.'

'Good to have that sorted. Wouldn't want an innocent person accused in the wrong.'

For a minute, she looked at me tight-lipped, then she laughed. It was the first time I had ever heard her laugh.

'Shell shock, it used to be called,' she said, as if she had to do a presentation on PTSD. 'Army guys in a war would get it. *Some* army guys. But it can develop outside combat in response to a traumatic event that overwhelms the person's sense of being in charge of their own life.'

What tended to distinguish the disorder from normal stress responses to a bad life event, she went on, were things like flashbacks, nightmares and symptoms of uncontrollably acute stress during flashbacks.

'Losing interest in normal living and feeling remote, emotionally. They're part of it, too.'

'And insomnia?'

'Yep. Very much so.'

She stood up and walked around the room and then came back and sat down.

'Adopting the medical model has its attractions,' she told me. 'Easiest thing in the world for me to get my GP to refer me to someone and get a prescription and treatment and so on. Why are you shaking your head?'

'That wouldn't be the easiest route for you. It wouldn't be easy for you at all – you bristled as much as if I'd questioned your personal integrity when I first mentioned PTSD. Your self-esteem would be damaged – you would be affronted by not being in charge. Very intelligent people often cause themselves a lot of problems by believing they're too clever to experience mental illness or disorders.'

'I don't think I'm too clever to be mentally ill. I think you're close to being right. But having some of the symptoms of PTSD – all right, *most* of the symptoms, doesn't mean I need a psychiatrist. And no, I don't think there's anything wrong with attending a psychiatrist, either. What I think is that it's possible to get into a series of vicious circles and I did. I've gone back to the gym, I haven't renewed the sleeping pill prescription and I've almost physically forced myself to – oh, Jesus, that Oprah Winfrey crap of living in the moment? I did a relaxation class so I can breathe when I get a panic attack. All right?'

This was asked with such aggression, all I could do was gesture: was it all right with her? She sighed.

'The nightmares are still there but not so much. I can be PTSD or I can be me somewhere other than bloody IBRC and that's my choice. I don't know what game you were playing when you raised post traumatic stress disorder – sorry,' she said, realising, without any overt reaction from me, that talk of playing games was not going to be helpful. 'Sorry. I don't care why you brought it up, because it gave me a useful jolt. Half the country's been made redundant. Fine. But I was one of the elite. One of the achievers. It isn't just my job that's been stripped away from me – it's my sense of who I am, what I'm worth. Because now, I know I'm worth nothing and that I was living in a myth. Well, that's where I've been for the past year. I honestly think Niall got past that sense of shame at least six months ago – the fact that he would casually go up to you in the street is evidence of that. Maybe because he did get another job although it's not at all what he should – it's not really at a level that properly uses his experience, his expertise. But he got it and it's one of the things that – I don't know – has moved him – moved him –'

'Further along the road to recovery?'

'Recovery from what?'

'You tell me.'

When she got tired of bristling, she grimaced. Maybe it was recovery from trauma. Or recession. Or something. It didn't really matter – the difference between them was that he had got himself somehow to a place where he could get into his suit and go to work at a job that utilised about half his skills and paid him half what he was worth, without his rage being at a constant low boil. Because that's the way he dealt with their new reality.

'Niall was hungry for a job and he didn't care how low on the totem pole that job was. Any job was acceptable to him if it would prevent him landing in the unemployed bracket. I should have followed his example at the time and picked up – '

'Nope,' I said. 'Niall's his own man. You're your own woman. Different people who just happen to be married to each other. Different personalities and make-up and neither of you needs to follow any example set by the other.'

'Fine, in that case here's where I'm at. I have been traumatised, yes. Am I suffering from PTSD? No. I may have come close but that was partly because I didn't have options. I know I want to do what I'm good at and earn money for it and if that means applying thousands of times (and never getting the courtesy of a response) or lining up in the street for a small possibility, I'll do it.'

A comment Eoghan had made in his *Irish Times* piece came back to me: 'It was once said of the dancing partners Fred Astaire and Ginger Rogers,' he wrote, 'that Ginger had to do everything Fred did – except backwards wearing high heels. It's going to be like that for former Anglo employees – they'll have to tailor their cover letters and CVs for each organisation that they're applying to and role they're applying for and prepare for interviews so that when the tapes question surfaces, they know how to handle it and when the tapes question *doesn't* surface, they know how to out it – and kill it.'

Yes, Jasmine said, she'd seen the piece and it had pushed her further along the route she was on. She was seeing Eoghan the following week for him to help her prepare for a job interview she was determined to ace. But she would be back to me after that, she said.

I shook hands with her and wished her well. I don't expect to see her again in a coaching session, mainly because she doesn't need to see me again; this will quickly become apparent to her and she'll see no point in doing more sessions just to be pleasant about it. Like someone thrown from a horse, she's got herself remounted, feet in stirrups, reins in hand. It may not be the best horse for her, it may be difficult to point it in the right direction and she may find the going tough in the short term but now, at least, Eoghan tells me, she's got the job she went for. That doesn't mean the endless fraught negotiations with banks will stop but it's akin to having joined the workforce in the first place. She has rejoined the normal workplace, like Niall, and every week, every month they put in at their less-than-perfect current posts puts clear blue water between the future they're aiming for and the past disaster they never caused.

CAREER PITFALL #3: BEING CRUSHED BY A FALLING (CELTIC) TIGER

This happens when the combination of your indebtedness, fallen income, negative equity and diminished career prospects leaves you with nothing but learned helplessness and a version of PTSD.

Five Tips for You as Your Own Coach

1. Ban mention of the past. Tell those around you that the minute you start talking about the bad advice that got you to where you now are, about rotten decisions, government, banks or developers, they're to say two words to you: 'future tense.' Nothing you can do about the past. No point in sitting in it upsetting yourself. Apart from removing generalised stench, one of the reasons we take a soiled nappy off a toddler is to prevent it getting a sore bottom. Sitting in the miseries of the past is the moral equivalent of a child left too long in a soiled nappy: you'll stink up the place and make yourself very sore.
2. Stop thinking 'when this is over.' Things are never going to be the way they were. You have to live with conditions the way they are. Right now.
3. Don't get precious when a bank employee says something you perceive as patronising. They've the job from hell. Be civil.
4. Explain your figures and what you can achieve to the bank. Keep your voice down. Stay civil. (See a pattern here?)

5. Help someone else. You're in no position? Nonsense. Someone needs something from you right now that you're too
   absorbed in your own miseries to notice. Notice them. Find
   time for them. Shut up and listen to them. Coach them. You
   know the old Biblical advice: 'Throw your bread upon the
   waters and it will return to you after many days'? Throw more
   than you think you have available, in time, in attention and in
   generosity, at someone else, and you will be astonished how
   rewarded you will be.

4

The Man Who Could Lie like a Rug

Elaine Anderson first came to me for coaching about eight years ago, returning once or twice a year since then when she has a problem or complex challenge she wants to talk out with someone outside her workplace. Now and then she books me to be part of a process so that I will be able to advise her on how to improve her management of that process. On this occasion, she asked me to be the outside member on a job interview panel along with herself and Adrian, the Head of HR, ready to interrogate three contenders for a major new role within the company.

Of the three, the youngest seemed to have most going for him. His name was Roger Birkin and he was due to be the third to be interviewed. Roger was tall, bearded and relaxed.

Adrian took him through his understanding of the to-be-created role. Roger was crisply confident, pointing to his 2:1 in electronic engineering by twenty-two and internship with one of the most forward-looking companies in Britain as evidence of his suitability.

'You were partly educated in Britain. Why was that?'

'My dad was a bank manager with AIB in Britain, so we spent time in several cities where the bank was represented. He doesn't work for the bank any more.'

Adrian and he then got into a patch of confusion as to where Roger had been at sixteen. Although Roger stayed calm, his face reddened with annoyance when he found he had contradicted himself. I couldn't see that it mattered very much but then I have but a loose grasp on decades, never mind individual years. After the Swinging Sixties, I can't distinguish one decade from another. So when someone says, 'That was *so* eighties,' I don't know whether they're on about mullets, Doc Martins, shoulder pads or disco floors. All I know is that it's a pejorative description. Oddly, any descriptor used to cover the last fifty years is pejorative. Our parents and grandparents talked of 'the twenties' or 'the thirties' with nostalgia: weren't we cute, all the same? That's been replaced, in our time, by 'What were we thinking?', which we use to sell ourselves down yesterday's river.

When the timelines had been semi-sorted, Adrian, who seemed to do a lot of totting in the margins of a CV, gestured that I should take over.

'Roger, what's the characteristic – the habit, the skill, the trait you have that you think particularly suits you for this job?'

Roger visibly relaxed and warmed to me.

'Passion,' he said firmly.

Another bloody passionist, I thought. I'm so sick of the over-use of the word passion. You have butchers these days butchering with passion, chocolatiers chocolating away with passion, wall-paperers wallpapering with passion. What passion has to do with it, I cannot see. If all you want is a lamb chop, a sticky toffee or wallpaper without bubbles in it, you don't care that much about the passionate commitment of the provider. Just what's provided.

'Let me explain,' Roger said, 'Because "passion" is too easy and obvious a word for what I mean.'

You're good, I thought. I'm pretty impassive but you none-theless picked up on my lack of enthusiasm for your passion. He then did a duck-and-weave around the issue which boiled down to an understanding that once he was on the job, you'd better be with him or you'd end up with track marks on your face.

'I had the privilege of meeting Steve Jobs before he died and he told me that focus was the single most important characteristic he looked for in new recruits.'

'How did you meet Steve Jobs?'

'He spoke at the John Lennon Conference Centre in Liverpool the year before he died and my company sent me. My own family has been affected by that particular cancer, so it was particularly moving to see him making such a great effort to overcome the discomfort and deliver with such warmth.'

Turning the pages of his CV, I noted that, in among multi-coloured belts for martial arts, he listed 'reading' as one of his pastimes.

'What book are you currently reading?'

He put a hand over his mouth and looked at the ceiling.

'Do you know something, I can see the cover of it but can't remember the title?'

'Author?'

'I'm really sorry.'

'Fiction or non-fiction?'

'Well, it would be sort of – it would be fiction.'

'Book you read before that one?'

If I had asked him how many under-age hedgehogs he had recently molested, he couldn't have been more embarrassed.

'I just read so many – I always have a book going, you know?'

'Don't worry about it, it really has nothing to do with your competences.'

I asked him a couple of scenario questions – the kind where you present a possible situation and ask people how they'd deal with it. His answers demonstrated the capacity to think quickly under pressure. Then Adrian and Elaine finished off the interview and he was shown down to Reception by Adrian. This allowed Elaine and me to have a brief exchange.

'Need to talk to you some more about the manner of questioning and how you listen but let's do that on another day, OK?' I said, just as Adrian arrived back into the room.

Elaine nodded and the two of them began to go through their (properly) weighted grid. Roger was better on almost all of the qualifying points than either of the other two.

'Terry, matter of interest, why'd you push him on what he was reading?' Adrian asked.

'Why do you think?'

'If it had been anybody other than Elaine's favourite consultant,' Adrian said, dodging the mock-blow Elaine aimed at him, 'I'd've thought you'd gone AWOL but – because Elaine swears by you –' ducking again, '– I gave you the benefit of the doubt.'

'And what did you come up with?'

'That you thought he was telling porkies.'

Elaine looked astonished.

'Now, many would suggest that telling porkies to cover up the fact that you're reading *Twenty Shades of Grey* shouldn't matter in a job interview...' Adrian trailed off, looking a question.

'Fifty,' Elaine said. '*Fifty Shades of Grey.*'

'Should it matter if someone lies about the book they're reading?' Adrian mulled it over.

'Everybody tells some white lies,' Elaine said. Adrian said nothing.

'Adrian?'

'I'm thinking.'

We waited.

'It *could* matter. It could. It could matter morally. But it might also matter in another way. You've got a CV of three pages. You choose what goes into it. If you – if you respect your prospective employer...Should you prepare...Look, Jasus, there's not that much in a CV, wouldn't kill him to – no, it's not about preparing. If it was true, he'd know.'

'Question,' I said. 'Have you gone through his credentials? His referees?'

'He saved us the trouble,' Adrian said, opening a folder to his right.' He actually sent them to us. Here.'

He handed two reference letters to me. I glanced at them and set them aside.

'Did you check his academic credentials or talk to his referees?'

Adrian now looked unhappy and impatient. He shook his head. Elaine just looked worried.

'The book question was the only one I could legitimately use to find out if he was lying. First thing that bothered me – and it may not have been a legitimate source of worry – was his comment about AIB. I know AIB was in Britain and may still be. Not sure it was in that many cities. Could be wrong. Not sure they had branches. Could be wrong. Not sure they moved managers around *those* branches, as opposed to bringing them back to Ireland. Could be wrong. But he got very antsy over where he was during some irrelevant period – why? So I asked him about the books and met a brick wall. He may have read a book at some stage but I doubt it. Not because of his answer but because of this.'

I lifted the first of the letters of reference. 'Reference from Keelin BioPharma. Alexander Coote. And another from –'

Adrian supplied the name of the company.

'How often does a job applicant present their letters of reference in advance of an interview?'

The two of them looked at each other and Elaine laughed. 'When he's extra eager? No. That's not going to cut it, is it?'

'Make a suggestion? Put me somewhere with coffee and spend the next hour checking a couples of things? First, check the degree. Second, check this reference but not that one. Thirdly, check with AIB – no, they'll never reveal –'

'Leave that to me,' Adrian said.

They put me in a room with lots of good coffee. When we regrouped, things were a fair bit clearer.

'We're done, he's done, it's over. He didn't get a 2:1. He got a degree but it sure as hell wasn't a 2:1,' Elaine said. 'I'm to get a call back about the reference but he wouldn't have got to this stage if it weren't for the degree, so he's done.'

'His father was never a manager in AIB in Britain,' Adrian said. 'I can't tell you how I know but trust me, I know.'

'We don't need to check the Keelin BioPharma reference,' Elaine said. 'Or do we?'

'I've done a lot of work for Keelin,' I said, 'and one of the fascinating things about them – I don't believe they would see this as commercially sensitive – one of the fascinating things is how they do references. They have a template. Let's say the reference is for you, Roger. Following the template, it'll say 'Roger Birkin worked in Keelin BioPharma from such-and-such a date to such-and-such a date as a microbiologist.' Or whatever role you had there. And that's it. They don't say the ex-employee was good, bad or indifferent. Ever. They've decided it's legally safer that way.'

'But wasn't Alexander Coote one of the founder directors of that firm? Rules that would apply to people further down the food chain mightn't apply to him,' Elaine said.

'You make a good point,' I said. 'And they definitely wouldn't apply to this reference, since he was dead when he wrote it.'

Adrian opened his folder and looked at his copy of the reference and then at me.

'It's dated 8 August 2011. I was at Alex's funeral a week before that. In the church in Booterstown opposite Gleeson's pub. Very sad.'

'Couldn't have met Steve Jobs, either,' Elaine said. 'I can't prove it yet but the biographical details on Jobs don't include him having been in the John Lennon Convention Centre at any time the year before he died. Our boy deserves the Booker prize for fiction. Our boy's talented as hell. Our boy's fantastic. Except for the small teeny tiny truth problem. I should get you to train our recruitment interviewers in how to spot liars,' she concluded.

'Or you could check credentials and references,' I said. 'Don't want to turn down your business but it'd be cheaper to start there.'

Companies should always follow up referees, asking for specific evidence for the generalised praise characteristic of most references. Only by asking for such evidence will a recruiter get to the truth of the former employer's view of their former employee. Some companies have taken to checking references *before* they do the interviews. Too often, though, the reverse is the case: companies fall in love with a job applicant and decide that they really don't need to do the background work on them. This isn't confined to the commercial world or to Ireland. A couple of overseas hospitals have ended up employing dangerously under-qualified or in some cases *un*qualified medical professionals in key functions because they didn't check that the individual's claimed qualifications were based on reality.

According to Robert Trivers, an academic who has studied the issue of lying, the young man who passed himself off as having a better electronics engineering degree than was the reality wouldn't have been exceptional in the level of his personal deceit.

'We are thoroughgoing liars, even to ourselves,' Trivers says. 'Our most prized possession – language – not only strengthens our ability to lie but greatly extends its range. We can lie about events distant in space and time, the details and meaning of the behaviour of others, our innermost thoughts and desires and so on. But why, why, *self*-deception? Why do we possess marvellous sense organs to detect information, only to distort it after arrival?'

Seems pretty bleeding obvious to me. We lie about ourselves because we prefer the version we make up to the one we grew up with. Doctors find that patients much prefer the version of themselves that's lighter than the one weighing down the scales in the surgery. Toupees and hair-replacement surgery sell to men who prefer the version of themselves that has much more hair than the one facing them in the bathroom mirror.

The most law-abiding and tax-compliant people lie out of

vanity and hope. But lies, for some people, are primarily stimulated not by a desire to live on Cloud 9 but by a desire to stay out of prison. Coco Chanel lied her way out of post-war suspicion of collaborating with the Nazis, although she had done much worse than collaborate. Her preferred lover during the war years was a Nazi spy whose association with her allowed him to hobnob with the influential, knowledgeable and powerful, picking up whatever crumbs might turn out to be useful to the Third Reich. Chanel lied about her past, her present and her business contracts and lived to a safe, cherished and wealthy old age on the proceeds.

A new book puts 'the little Sparrow', Edith Piaf, right up there beside Chanel as a woman who could and did lie like a rug.

'Piaf's duplicity was without limits,' says Robert Belleret, the book's author. Having gone through contemporaneous documentation, Belleret maintains the singer liked lying so much, she even fibbed about where she was born, claiming that her mother gave birth to her in a Paris street whereas she was in fact born – like almost everybody else – in a hospital. It's the 'like almost everybody else' bit that matters, here. Piaf's confected life was much more interesting to herself and to others than her real life, even though that was impelling in its squalor. Earlier biographers have suggested that the washing of clothing held no charm for Piaf. She bought clothes – underwear and outerwear – when it struck her to do so and then wore the garments until they became too disgusting for her to continue in them. At which point she threw them away and bought replacements.

Although she may not have been as ruthlessly exploitative of wartime possibilities as was Churchill's friend Coco, Edith Piaf nonetheless had a grubby war, living over a brothel patronised by Nazi VIPs. Grubby but suspiciously well-fed, which landed her in front of one of the investigations set up to identify collaborators. A collaborator? *Moi*? Well, of course she was but she sold the investigators a yarn about her fearlessly helping hundreds of prisoners to escape occupied France. None of the hundreds who owed their lives to her ever came forward during or after her lifetime to thank her for it. Funny, that.

One of the functions of biography, these days, seems to be exposing just how good at lying famous figures of the past could be and how lamentably bad their contemporaries were when it came to catching them at it. This seems to point, first of all, to the 'halo effect' generated by fame. Chanel and Piaf, in their own lifetimes, were seen as French national treasures, and it's much easier to believe those you know and venerate than it may be to believe complete strangers. Both had difficult childhoods, albeit perhaps not as difficult as they painted it in adulthood. People tend to make allowances for those who have come through cruelty or deprivation and believe their stories, as if the very incoherence of these stories was in itself a proof of their veracity.

The real reason they got away with it, however, is a simple fact: human beings are lousy at spotting lies and they complicate this deficit by kidding themselves to the contrary. Most people believe they're good at spotting when others are lying. Journalists and cops are convinced they're *fantastic* at it. Delusions of grandeur. Stan Walters, 'the lie guy' who trains American cops and FBI agents in interrogation, says that his experiments show that police officers are only as good as the average person at spotting untruths. Adrian and Elaine nailed this spectacular liar because they checked the obvious in a way many companies don't – they didn't spot Roger, through personality traits, as a pathological liar. You don't have to be specially trained to catch liars. They rarely pay enough attention to detail to protect themselves from discovery. They get away with it because other people pay even less attention.

CAREER PITFALL #4: LYING LIKE A RUG

Psychopaths, as Elaine found out, lie all the time and have not the smallest remorse when caught out. If you work in HR, you need to watch out for them – and also for the ordinary decent job applicants who lie on their CV or job interview to cover up something of which they're ashamed.

Five Tips for You as Your Own Coach

1. If you've done something you figure might be a disadvantage in a job for which you've applied, think twice about glossing over it in your CV. Well-trained recruitment interviewers are likely to work out that there's something fishy in the sequence. The same applies in your job interview. You don't have to be confessional but if you're setting out to be a trusted employee, it helps to be trustworthy, so offering up the fact that you had to do one exam twice and giving the reason for it may be a better option than letting on that you got through all exams first time and with flying colours.

2. Never lie to make yourself look more on top of a job than you are. If you're in trouble, ask for help. Colleagues are flattered, not affronted, when asked for advice or a leg-up.

3. Never lie to cover up a mistake. It's the wrong thing to do and if you're found out, it will complicate the original error, diminish other people's trust in you and damage your reputation.

4. Above all, don't lie to yourself. If you know you're no good at something or have made a mistake or perhaps done worse than a mistake, kidding yourself to the contrary is asinine.

5. If you're on the other side of the equation: in the interviewing panel, get yourself trained so that you know how to interview rigorously and capture information offered in order to select the candidate who's genuinely best for the job.

5

Wired but Not Connected

Nobody does an eye-roll like Stephanie Brady, our Chief Operating Officer. That's a title that allows us to ask her to do anything, which we do and which she does. So on this lovely morning, the cherry trees outside dappled with sunshine, she's at her desk taking to a client who should at that moment be in the Marcus room with me discussing her career but who, we gather by eavesdropping on Steph's conversation, is in fact at our old premises in Northumberland Road. Steph tells her how to get to us. Describes our new premises. You literally can't miss it. It's a brick Byzantine building opposite the Royal Victoria Eye and Ear Hospital on Adelaide Road. Until it was deconsecrated more than a decade ago, it was the capital city's oldest synagogue.

'Is she going to find us?' someone asked Steph as she put down the phone. The response was a head shake which turned out to be correct. The client made an energetic attempt to convince the Presbyterian Church just down the road that *it* was the synagogue but Presbyterians don't convert that easily. By the time she was seated in the Marcus room (we named all the meeting rooms after Dublin Jews prominent in the arts: David Marcus, Harry Kernoff and Louis Elliman) half an hour of her time was gone, although she seemed to be in high good humour about it.

'I'm really sorry, Tracy,' she told me, 'but I was actually able to do a few phone calls that were very important.'

'Terry,' I corrected. 'Right, let's make the best use of our time. Why're you here?'

'My mother's a huge fan of yours.'

I waited for the second shoe to fall.

'And my granny. My granny thinks you're great.'

She seemed to think this was enough to be getting on with and got distracted by something on her smart phone. After a second, she looked up at me with that wide-eyed startled gaze characteristic of someone who thinks it's your conversational turn rather than their conversational turn. I smiled at her and said nothing.

She finished off what she was doing on the phone and told me where she worked – a small generics-producing pharmaceutical company. She'd been there for two weeks, she said, as her phone rang. She stuck it to her ear and made apologetic gestures while heading to the door, apparently intending to take the call on the landing. I drank coffee for five minutes. After three the conversation outside stopped but she didn't come back in – and when she did, she was looking at the screen of the phone in dismay. Tears in her eyes, she held the phone out to me. On the screen was a tweet aimed at her which suggested she was too stupid to live and recommending how she might end her life.

'You've been in your job two weeks?' I prompted. The phone went off again. This time she told the caller she was in a meeting and would call them back.

'Sorry, Tracy.'

'Terry. You've been in your job two weeks?'

'I'm desperate with names,' she announced. It seemed to be a source of simple pride to her.

'You've been in your job two weeks?'

Something flashed on the phone and her index finger rose, ready to type.

'Turn it off.'

'Sorry?'

'Turn it off. You're paying a lot of money for this session. You can't afford to waste that money.'

'I'm grand,' she said, typing. 'I'm brilliant at multi-tasking.'

At which point she overturned the milk jug. I had never noticed, up to then, that our boardroom table is divided into multiple sections, which allowed the milk to pour onto the carpet in thin and varied streams. I left the room to get damp tea-towels while she wrote her emails. Order restored, I sat down. She poured from the replacement jug, announcing that she probably should have asked for peppermint tea.

'You've been in the job two weeks?'

The phone went off again. I reached across, took it, turned it off and put it beside me. Her expression belonged in that Jacques Louis David painting, *The Rape of the Sabine Women*.

'I can't be out of contact,' she said. 'Say if there was an emergency? No, seriously, I can't. I'm a brilliant – '

'Multi-tasker,' I finished. 'No such thing.'

'No, honestly, I have to have it on.'

'No problem.'

I slid the phone across the table to her. It moved more slowly than I'd expected, I suspect because the table was still damp with spilt milk. Over which little Ms Multi-tasker might cry, it seemed.

'I suppose I could turn it off for ten minutes if you really want me to,' she said, like she was conceding Alsace and Lorraine.

'Thirty minutes remain in your session.'

The phone went off again. She had instinctively turned the power back on. As she headed for the door, she put a hand over the mouthpiece bit of the phone to hiss at me that this call was really important and she absolutely had to take it. I sat there, drinking coffee. It's lucky I like coffee, I get so many unplanned opportunities to imbibe it.

The door opened and one of my colleagues entered the meeting room. 'First time I ever saw a client spend more time on the landing than in the meeting room,' he said.

'Clients are *so* interesting,' I said. 'I think she thinks I'm Tracy Piggott.'

He looked at me with insulting disbelief and said that quite apart from – as he euphemistically put it – not being Tracy Piggott's age, I knew damn all about horse racing.

'Your client picks holes in the plaster, that's what I came in to tell you,' he said, losing interest in Tracy and horse racing.

'How d'you mean?'

He mimed being on the phone while picking bits out of the wall with a bent over index finger.

'For fecksake,' I said. 'The plaster's only *there* eight weeks.'

'Well, the wall outside looks as if someone took a very small ice-pick to it.'

The client came back into the room. My colleague ducked his head at her and headed past her in the doorway.

'See ya, Tracy,' he called over his shoulder and I made a resolution to slice, dice and fry him later that day.

'You're two weeks on the job?' I said. '*In* the job, I mean. *In* the job.'

She began to poke at the nail of her index finger with a pen. That's our wall plaster you have in there, I thought.

'Two years,' she said, quite crossly. 'I told you that.'

'All right,' I said equably. 'What's your job like?'

She looked at the screen of the phone as if it held the answer. Very busy, she said. You know yourself the price of branded pharmaceuticals. While I was trying to work that one out, she said that her father had been in charge of the generics plant a big pharma company had set up in a satellite town on the northside of Dublin, and when the big pharma company decided that making their own generics didn't make as much sense as they'd thought it would, her father had put together a consortium to buy it and they had.

At this point, Stephanie came in the door with a folded half

A4 sheet bearing the message: 'Your next client is in the Kernoff Room and Anton is waiting to come into this room with his client.'

'I know, I know, we're out of time,' the young woman said. 'That's fine. I've got *so* much out of this session, you wouldn't believe. You might think I wouldn't pick up your good advice but I really am a multi-tasker.'

I watched her head out into the sunshine, wondering how a bright young graduate could convince herself that she'd just had a productive meeting when the sum total of nothing had been achieved. I assumed I'd never see her again. After all, she was sitting pretty in Daddy's firm so she could be as distracted as she wanted to be. I was startled when she bounced back the following week. Or maybe 'bounced back' would be putting it too positively. She made an urgent appointment and when she arrived, handed over her phone to HaiYing, who met her at the front door. HaiYing has a smile she reserves for when Irish people do something that makes no sense to a decent Chinese woman from Dalian. She gave Deborah, our client, a smile implying that all our clients hand their phones over to her on arrival – even though this was a first – and took her upstairs.

'Hi, Deborah,' I greeted the now telephone-free client.

'Hi, Ms Prone,' was the response.

I laughed. It was more accurate than 'Tracy' but a surprise, nonetheless.

'Why're we gone so formal?'

'I had a debriefing.'

'Yeah?'

'With my father. He made me take him through what happened last week, minute by minute.'

'And?'

'He was very disappointed.'

Someone arrived with coffee for me and peppermint tea for Deborah. This seemed to upset her. 'I thought you said you'd have preferred peppermint tea the last day?'

'Oh, it's lovely, it's just you remembered and that's what my father said. I thought he just wanted me to – well, really I thought in the beginning that he was going along with my mother because for her me meeting you would be the next best thing to meeting you herself, she likes you so much.'

Please, I thought silently, don't let's involve the granny in this. Leave your granny out of it.

'But he says that was just handy – my mother being a fan – that he wanted me to – to – get fixed.'

Deborah was now as fidgety as if she needed a coke top-up. She seemed on the verge of standing up, of walking out. Then she took the china cup of peppermint tea in both hands and drank it, sip by sip, as if she was counting each minty swallow. When the cup was empty, she put it down carefully and put both her hands in her lap like a Victorian schoolgirl.

'He said I was driving him out of his fucking tree,' she said, and burst into tears. I shoved a box of tissues across the table to her and she mopped herself, blew her nose and then touchingly shoved the balled-up tissue up her sleeve.

'How?'

'He said I was like a mental defective, no offence, but that's the word he actually used and when I said a person with an intellectual disability he said, "That too." He never in my whole life, *never…*'

As the tears started again, she retrieved the balled-up tissues from her sleeve and I wondered whence that odd strand of thriftiness came. Using it gave her the appearance of rolling a small snowball around her face.

'Let's go back a bit,' I said. 'Where do you come in your family?'

'It's just me. I'm an only child, I mean.'

'How much do you like your parents?'

'Oh, they're the best. We're really close. I was really hoping when the CAO – you know? Yeah. When I was filling out the form, I was dreading I might end up in Galway or somewhere and have to live away from home. We're really close.'

'Which are you closest to, your mum or your dad?'

'My dad but that's not saying – I don't mean, I really…with my mum it's like we're sisters. '

'Does your father want you to take over the company?'

The wet ball of tissues went up the sleeve again and down came the two small hands into her lap.

'My father would want whatever made me happy.'

'Does your father want you to take over the company?'

'Well, if I was good enough and if I like wanted to.'

'You got a degree. What age are you?'

'Twenty-five.'

That surprised me. I had thought her around the twenty-two mark.

'I know what you're thinking,' she said. (Funny thing, when people say they know what you're thinking. They're almost never right but it invariably leads them to an important self-revelation.)

'I failed first year and I failed my finals and had to repeat. My father has three degrees,' she added.

'Good for him,' I said dismissively. 'Why'd it take you so long to get yours?'

'I don't really know.'

'Yeah, you do.'

'Just.'

'Just what?'

'It was harder than I thought.'

'Why?'

'There was other stuff going on.'

Deborah went back to fidgeting – de-pilling the ribbing at the wrist of her cardie. I was trying to work out how to find out if she was intellectually foundering. Or had been while in college.

'Every student has a social life.'

Another long silence. 'Didn't you?'

'Have a social life in university? God, no. I wasn't attractive enough for anyone to want to have a social life with me. Anyway, I'm a drop-out. Lasted a year.'

'*Really?*'

She was looking at me as if it came as a surprise to her that someone without a degree could walk upright and drink from a cup, never mind run a company or write a book. It seemed to come as a great relief to her. Sort of reverse credentialism.

'I always thought I was doing better than I was, to be perfectly honest with you,' she confessed. 'My father had me tested at one stage.'

'For what?'

'Intelligence.' A gust of laughter came out of her. 'To see did I have any.'

'Did you?'

'Yeah. I was above average but not genius. My father is a genius. He could be in Mensa if he wanted but he wouldn't want to. He thinks they're a naval-gazing shower of freak-show shites.'

'That a quote?'

'Sorry?'

'Did *he* call them freak-show shites?'

'Yes.'

'I like the sound of your father.'

'You'd love him. He's the best at everything he does. Everything he ever did. I want him to be proud of me.'

'For what?'

'For not faffing and farting around and wasting my bloody time.'

'That another quote from him?'

She nodded, solemnly.

'So it's not that he wants you to run the company or get a great degree or – '

'Oh, no, he wants me to be happy whatever way I want. I just drive him batshit crazy not concentrating.'

'Always?'

'How do – oh, like as a child? Like ADHD? No. Maybe a bit but I was never on pills.'

I wondered but not aloud, if this was because she had two parents devoted to her with no competition from siblings, intelligent enough to work on strategies to keep their young one focused without pharmaceutical help.

'He's been getting mad in the last few months and I thought the way he was it was just that he was getting old. You know? Like you'd expect him not to be into Twitter or Facebook although the company does have a page and to be honest with you he does have a Nook for reading books because it's easier on him when he's travelling not to be carrying a whole lot of books. I said to him he should put the books on his iPad and there'd be links to stuff and he just closed down his machine and went for a walk. When he came back he said to me that he wanted me to go and meet a woman who'd run a business and listen to her and that's why I was here last week but you see, I didn't know, I really didn't know that he thought I was fragmenting my mind and that meeting you would stop me, give me a proper role model maybe and then he found out, I mean I told him honestly about going to the wrong place and spilling the coffee and not being good with names. He said crap, he'd told me all about you and me being on the phone was ridiculous and I was to give it up the minute I arrived. I did, too.'

'I have to hand it to your father, I've got much more out of this session than I did out of the last one because your phone couldn't interrupt you. How did he not expect you to be using your phone? I mean, does he not see you using it all the time at work?'

Mobile phone use was not permitted at all in her father's plant because it did manufacturing of small molecules and there'd be the danger of a spark or fire. I nodded as if I understood this.

'When you come in first thing you hand your phone over to the receptionist,' Deborah said. 'From then on, everybody operates on landlines.'

'And you manage?'

'Well, I have my iPad for Facebook and texts and tweets.'

'Deborah?'

'Yes?'

'Keep your knee still and stop doing that.'

If I had struck her, backhanded, across the face, she couldn't have looked more hurt. Instinctively, she reached out to scoop dozens of tiny rolled-up shreds of tissue from in front of her. I put my hand out: no.

'What do they mean?'

'Nothing.'

'Every move we make, every word we utter has significance. Whether we intend it to or not. Now, what's the significance of that little lot?'

'My hands are usually occupied so when I'm sitting doing nothing…That's one of the things my father said. He said I should've played camogie.'

I narrowed my eyes, trying to get a fix on the connection I was sure existed between the two statements.

'Yeah. No, he says I'm desperate at meetings. But that's just because he used to be great at sport. Hurling, you know? He says if you've trained to be an athlete, your body knows not to be wasting time fidgeting. Is that true?'

'Haven't a clue. But I like the idea. What do you do at meetings?'

This one stumped her. Her right knee provided a silent, repetitive and unintended answer and I decided that asking her again to control it might be a bit much. After a while, she told a story which became almost funny, about gradually having things taken from her at meetings because she was using them to drive fellow participants out of their minds. The list included pens with clicky ends, notebooks belted with elastic bands to hold them closed, loose rubber bands and paperclips. She also, she confessed, sometimes found herself flicking the top corner of her diary with a forefinger.

'If I could have my phone with me at meetings, I'd be grand,' she said. 'Everybody'd be grand. I wouldn't need to do other things. Well, OK, maybe I don't *need* to do other things. My father says it's like giving up smoking.'

This *non-sequitur* made me worry that this young woman might have some mild version of Tourette's Syndrome, a worry exacerbated by the speed at which her knee was jiggling. A tiny mad part of my mind was trying to invent a power-capture mechanism which could be used to harness the energy she expended in the fastest repetitive movements found outside a sub-machine gun.

'He says if you've been a chain smoker, you don't know what to be doing with your hands when you quit and it's sort of the same with the telephone.'

Deborah's father sounded like a man who watched other people, whereas it was emerging that his daughter didn't really watch people. Instead, she watched screens. The screen of her smart phone, the screen of her iPad, the screen of her laptop. Not the screen of her TV – whenever she wanted to see a TV programme, she watched it on her computer, commenting to friends all the time. Without technology connecting her with others, she had no idea what to do with her hands.

But that was the least of her worries. As we continued our coaching sessions over the ensuing months, Deborah was shocked to realise that although she was in constant electronic *contact* with huge numbers of acquaintances on issues of no great moment but transient gossip value, she hardly knew the people surrounding her in her own business. Some of her insights came about by analysing her day-to-day interactions but her father, a Type A personality if ever there was one, landed her face-down into some of them.

He brought her with him to a meeting in the procurement section of the health service. She was quite pleased and made sure to ask a few intelligent questions and get the names of those present correct. About a week after the meeting, her father called her into his tiny office and asked her what she had done, arising out of the encounter. Deborah was puzzled. He hadn't asked her to do anything, had he? Her father's response was to ask her if she thought she was still in primary school where someone older than you was always ready to tell you what to do, every hour of every day, or was she a senior executive in a small company that was under pressure because of the recession and the government's austerity policies.

Two days after that encounter, she turned up for a session with me that had been booked before her father had uttered.

'I need to go back to him with a solution,' she said.

'And it is?'

'I don't know. I can't remember what happened at the meeting. It didn't seem very important. I mean, procurement. Lots of dis-cussion of technical stuff and how they evaluate new drugs and that's not really going to affect us, because we're not at the innovation end of things.'

'Where are your notes?'

'What notes?'

What would have been the point of making notes, she wanted to know, when she'd never been at one of those meetings before and how, accordingly, could she judge what was important and what wasn't? A good question, I said. She looked at me, head on one side like a blackbird listening for worms.

'I could have asked Dad beforehand.'

I looked interested, as a worm would.

'We went in his car.'

She put her head in her hands and looked at me through her fingers. 'You know what I did all the way in to that meeting? I fixed his frigging Parrot. Programmed it so he could just call out names and it would dial them. He was very grateful,' she added resentfully.

'I'm sure he was,' I agreed.

'But you're telling me I should've been asking him all about the meeting and the people who were going to be at it and why they mattered and which of them had influence over the decisions made in the procurement area and what I should look out for and make notes of instead of sitting like a spare spanner?'

'I'm not telling you that.'

'Sor – Oh, right. *I'm* telling it to myself. Isn't my father rotten not to tell me? Wouldn't have killed him. Setting me up.'

I reminded her that she had decided she needed to go back to him with a solution. She sat and thought about this for a long time.

'No,' she said, straightening up and tidying her property for departure. 'No. Not with a solution. I just need to tell him I'm sorry.'

'Must try harder?'

She looked blank.

'That's what they used to put in school reports,' I said.

And that's what she did. She just tried harder. From then on, in preparation for any meeting, inside or outside the plant where she worked, she would talk to her father or to whoever had called the meeting in order to get a sense of what was to be achieved. At the meeting, she would make notes. Afterwards, she would follow up. In the process, she began to notice and find interesting the people around her. In consequence, it was she who registered the slight tremor in the left hand of one of the chemical engineers, a contemporary of her father.

'I told my dad and he thought I was imagining it. Then one day he spotted it for himself and he was so sad. But it meant that he was able to find ways to let Gerard talk to him about the Parkinson's so it stopped being a secret. And when Gerard needed to change slightly what he was doing at work, my father was way ahead of him and had it all sorted, no problem.'

Before the year was out, Deborah's mother had inadvertently paid her daughter the most welcome compliment ever. Listening to Deb recounting a conversation at work, her mother laughed.

'You're turning into your father,' she said.

Deborah was thrilled by the comment and even more thrilled to tell me how appalled she had been, the previous Friday evening, in the trendy pub favoured by her work colleagues, to find all seven of them, for almost an hour, doing nothing but addressing their smartphones, despite the fact that they were surrounded by people they would describe as a) interesting and b) friends.

'It's like I've left that stage behind me,' she concluded.

The great thing about spending measurably less time on social media is that, as well as improving Deborah's work performance, it's also likely to improve her happiness. A psychological study published in *Public Library of Science ONE* in 2013 found that the more frequently you visit Facebook, the worse you're likely to feel, whereas talking to friends in person or the phone makes you feel better. The study was directed by the University of Michigan in the US and its leader, Ethan Kross, said that yes, on the surface, Facebook provides an invaluable resource for fulfilling the basic human need for social connection.

'But rather than enhance wellbeing,' Kross observed, 'we found that Facebook use predicts the opposite result – it undermines it.'

In other words, social media provide connections, not necessarily *connectedness*.

CAREER PITFALL #5: BEING WIRED, NOT CONNECTED
'Multi-tasking' is the euphemism used to convince people that trying to do several things at once is not the Godawful waste of time it actually is.

Whoever invented the concept of multi-tasking is the spawn of Satan. Every useful bit of research says multi-tasking varies between pointless and dangerous. The Road Safety Authority, in common with all such agencies, worldwide, can produce a rake of studies proving that – no matter what drivers believe – they cannot drive and text simultaneously. The graveyards are home to a large number of people who were convinced that texting took only a split second and that this particular text was of life-and-death significance, whereas in fact it was only of death significance.

I'm thinking of writing a song for those deluding themselves that they're successfully juggling a multiplicity of tasks. To help them kick their counterproductive habit. I'm going to call it *One Thing at a Time, Sweet Jesus....*

Five Tips for You as Your Own Coach

1. Be super sensitive to any mention, in your annual or semi-annual appraisals of 'lack of focus', 'incapacity to follow up' or 'distractability'. Any one of these may be an indicator that your boss sees you as unable to concentrate and as flitting inattentively between tasks, achieving little in the process. Watch the people around you. The successful ones tend to be the ones who are not up-to-date on Twitter gossip and who have missed the latest video of a charming kitten falling uninjured out of a tree. These are the aspects of your life which may be admirably up to date if you're a social media fan. They're not necessarily what can be of most use in your place of work. When using social media like Twitter, don't kid yourself as to why you're on it. You just go on it every hour because that's where the best news updates are, right? Who're you kidding?

2. Sometimes, multi-tasking is an inevitability in any life, particularly when small children join the party. American writer Meg Wolitzer reminisced about this experience with the *Guardian's*

Emma Brockes. Married to another writer, she said that the two of them were proud of splitting the parenting tasks. 'If someone had a deadline and there was a vomiting child, the non-deadline person was hands on,' Wolitzer remembered. 'Looking back, there was a lot of half-parenting, too, which is when you're really distracted and you crave to be at your book but you're playing Cluedo; so both the game and that paragraph come out mediocre. It doesn't really work.'

Nobody with an eye on a rewarding career should ever try to do two things at once.

3. Understand that reading on a computer is not the same as reading a bound book. When you choose to download and read a book online, or, indeed, when you read prose on a blog or in Wikipedia, you enter a fairground of competing interruptions, all dressed up as added value. Try this on for size, from *The Shallows*, a book by Nicholas Carr that examines what the Internet is doing to our brains:

'A page of online text viewed through a computer screen may seem similar to a page of printed text. But scrolling or clicking through a Web document involves physical actions and sensory stimuli very different from those involved in holding and turning the pages of a book or magazine. Research has shown that the cognitive act of reading draws not just on our sense of sight but also on our sense of touch. It's tactile as well as visual…the shift from paper to screen doesn't just change the way we navigate a piece of writing. It also influences the degree of attention we devote to it and the depth of our immersion in it.

'Hyperlinks also alter our experience of media. Links are in one sense a variation on the textual allusions, citations and footnotes that have long been common elements of documents. But their effect on us as we read is not at all the same. Links don't just point us to related or supplemental works; they propel us toward them. They encourage us to dip in and out of a series of texts rather than devote sustained attention to any one of them. Hyperlinks are designed to grab our attention. Their value as navigational tools is inextricable from the distraction they cause...The searchability of online works also represents a variant on older navigational aids such as tables of contents, indexes and concordances. But here, too, the effects are different. As with links, the ease and ready availability of searching make it much simpler to jump between digital documents than it ever was to jump between printed ones. Our attachment to any one text becomes more tenuous, more provisional. Searches also lead to the fragmentation of online works. A search engine often draws our attention to a particular snippet of text, a few words or sentences that have strong relevance to whatever we're searching for at the moment, while providing little incentive for taking in the work as a whole. We don't see the forest when we search the Web. We don't even see the trees. We see twigs and leaves.'

4. Ask people around you if you have habits that drive them spare. If it emerges that one of them is a jigging limb, along the lines of Deborah's leg, and if, after you've been alerted to it, you still find it difficult to keep it still, here's a practical suggestion. Buy yourself strap-on weights. Strap a couple to your ankle or knee if you're wearing trousers. They'll serve as a reminder to your muscles, forcing them to work twice as hard if they want to start bounding around. They won't eliminate a bad habit quickly. It takes a long, long time to build up reflexes to replace those currently in operation. But it's worth it. Come on, you don't ever want to be so associated with a physical tic that when someone describes you to someone else who doesn't know you they use the tic as the central, the defining characteristic.

5. Create your own habits of concentration. Teach yourself to do one single thing at a time. Like read a book for fifteen minutes without answering the phone, a text, tweet or email. And without looking anything up on the internet. It won't be easy the first time, if you're normally a multi-tasker. What become our best habits (listening to people, taking exercise or being on time) are often quite problematic the first few times. Psychologist William James wrote in the nineteenth century about habits as allowing us to 'do a thing with difficulty the first time but soon do it more and more easily and finally, with sufficient practice, to do it semi-mechanically, or with hardly any consciousness at all…just as a sheet of paper or a coat, once creased or folded, tends to fall forever afterward into the same identical folds.'

6

The Man Who Could Talk for Europe

The title of this chapter describes a man who was and is a great talker. Our first coaching session usually hinges on a lengthy personal interview, which may or may not be recorded. This one was. And transcribed. So we can listen to him for a while as he outlined, on his first visit, what he wanted to achieve.

'Throughout my years as a manager, I've always held that a company's people are its greatest asset, so I would be positive when your name came up. Aside, of course, from the pleasure of telling my lovely wife that you are as glamorous in person as you are on the television. I would look forward to any tips and tricks you might give me that might improve my communication. I do a fair amount of public speaking, going back to being President of the L&H in UCD. We were the generation after Adrian Hardiman and without being excessive, it would be true to say that in addition to debating, we would be recognised as the generation that effectively created the Celtic Tiger.

Of course with that came some unfortunate spin offs, although I have to say that this demonising of people like [*he named a banker*] and [*he named a now-notorious banker*] has gone too far. I know those guys and they were the ones with vision enough to cut through bureaucracy in order to stimulate the economy. Of course, it's not politically correct to say that now but I remember the day when people who currently excoriate them would have been fawning on them. But that's always the way, isn't it? I always say that you should take care to be kind to people as you go up the ladder, because you will meet them on your way down the ladder.

'Why am I here? Well, as I said, my company invests in its people. Ten years ago, I attended the leadership programme in Harvard. You may have read about Brian Cowen also doing it? There's another man unfairly – in my view, it's just a personal opinion – unfairly treated by media. I had the honour of working with him; in fact, he appointed me to a state board and I always felt he was the right man in the right place. He was very clever but who can cope with a completely unprecedented situation, which was what he had to deal with? Media makes the assumption that he could have foreseen the hard landing of the property market but as I always say to younger people in my office, you must never assume anything. I write it down for them, the word 'assume,' like this and then I draw a line here and another here and I tell them, 'Whenever you assume,' I tell them, 'you make an ass out of you and me.' It's one of the things that I tell them will always stand to them.

'I've always, no matter how busy I might be at any given time, I've always done what you might call management by walking about. I have always found that staff appreciate that. Even the most junior person can gain from a bit of mentoring. That's a point I made very strongly to the President of Barrisco when they acquired the remaining equity in our firm – yes, they took it over. In 2003, actually. I remember that because I said at the time that it might be the first overseas investment of that scale coming out of the homeland. I always call it that when communicating with the Yanks. They love that word. They really do and you know the old axiom that when in Rome, do as the Romans do?

'It's one of the things I mean to do, if I get a little more time for myself in the future, is learn Italian. Beautiful language and of course I did Latin in Belvedere. However, *ars longa, vita brevis*[*]

---

[*] Art is long, life is short.

as you know. Given that Latin is the root of Italian, I expect it to be relatively easy to develop a level of verbal fluency that would enable me to engage conversationally when on holiday. My lovely wife loves Italy so much, she makes her own pasta from scratch. One of the little ones in my department has an Italian father. I can't remember her name but the surname is something like one of the ice-cream vans. Cafolla or something like that. I often mean to ask her where in Italy her father hails from and how he ended up in Ireland.

'Oh, yes, that's quite correct, you did ask me about the goals and objectives of this coaching exercise and quite properly, too. I must tell you we share that. In the past, when we were recruiting and I would be asked to participate on an interview panel – I suppose, if I'm to be honest with you, HR would want a bit of seniority, a bit of gravitas on the panel – I would always make sure to sit down with the other members of the panel. Nothing lengthy, just a cup of coffee and a chance to share our approach so that there was coherence, although it must be said that some of the modern systems of asking each job applicant exactly the same question is ludicrous. I told HR, I told them, 'This may be the flavour of the month coming from some MBA course but I'm a great believer in trusting your instinct and going with the question that strikes you or presenting the applicant with your opinion to see if they agree with it.' But then, HR has become so politically-correct, the constraints in recent times…the last time, I remember exactly when it was. It was the week of 20 February 2006. The post was in Technical Support but why I remember it – although I have to tell you I have a good memory, very little escapes me and you'll be glad to know I'm not dependent on gadgetry to remember things for me – why I remember it is because the new Head of Human Resources at the time held a meeting on the morning of the interviews, which was, I told her, very admirable. I always believe in encouraging juniors.

'I would not go so far as to say I found offensive some of the pointers she presented to us in the course of that preparatory meeting but I did point out to her that if we obeyed all of them, it would rob us of any but the questions any junior could ask. But of course she had her own agenda. Signs on it, she's in the Peoria plant now. It's three times the size of our Irish operation. She was made Vice-President in charge of human resources and when I sent a handwritten letter of congratulation I reminded her to be flexible, rather than ruled by manuals devoted to political correctness. Well, why should any company in tough times take on a woman of – of – a woman in her childbearing years when they could take a man of the same age? I am not a chauvinist but you must admit, in fairness, that there's a lot of abuse out there. Oh, you must. Women taking an extended holiday called maternity leave? Six months on full pay and the girl never turns up in the office during that time and never as much as lifts the phone to keep abreast of projects where she was part of the lead team. Six months on full pay if you're a multinational, that is.

I opened my mouth to interrupt at this point but got nowhere. He tacked on.

'Wouldn't it be interesting to find out how many women take six months or longer if they work for companies that don't pay maternity leave, where you're just on statutory? I suspect those statistics might be *very* interesting indeed. Very interesting indeed. Money talks, you know. That's what my father always said. Money talks. Money talks, it really does.

'Then they come back and – I'm not telling you anything you don't already know, you have to read the newspapers in your business – complain that they're on the mummy track and not promoted. Three or four years after they've become permanent and pensionable, they time it *so* carefully, they get pregnant and disappear for the guts of a year. That's assuming they have no complications during the pregnancy and I would conservatively estimate that 50 per cent of them have such complications, because all the services are there, lined up waiting to be accessed. Then they come back for a year or so, during which they are incessantly absent – incessantly – because the kid has an earache or a tummy ache. Then they get pregnant again and the same thing happens. I never get to learn the names of the young ones acting up – that's what they call it – 'acting up' – or the ones who get brought in on short-term contracts to replace the fertile females, as I call them.

'And you can't ask them, when they come back the second time, having disrupted their area for as long as four years and cost the company a financial fortune, you can't ask them, you're not *permitted* to ask them, in fact there is a *manual* on the *shelf* or rather on that thing, on your desktop, formally warning you *against* asking them if they're planning to do it again. I always say that the women's libbers brought in the politically correct era and prevented managers from managing. With the exception of Michael O'Leary. I might have reservations about some of the advertisements that Ryanair put in the newspapers about the Pope but he has his head screwed on the right way. When I heard the air hostesses on Ryanair sleep in their clothes – not the jacket, obviously, or the skirt or shoes – so that they can move quickly if the office wants to book them for a flight, I thought, "Great." I did. That's what I thought. "Great." If you don't want to do it, someone else does.

'But I was told – I was *instructed* by someone who at that time was considerably junior to me and younger by perhaps a decade – *instructed* not to ask, even in the perfectly acceptable, perfectly appropriate way I had planned, *instructed* not to ask if the young woman was going to have more children, even though, as I pointed out to her quite forcefully, the information this question would glean would inform important corporate plans. In other words, why would we, the panel, recommend that this girl who has already shown her priorities twice now be made a member of a major project team if we had no guarantee that she wouldn't be absent for more than half the duration of the project? I said we would have to agree to differ and that was fine until at lunchtime, the same day, I received an e-mail from the VP to whom I report or reported at the time – he's retired since – saying that I would not be required for that interview panel after all. This man was in Tobago.'

'What's the significance of his location? I asked.

'I'll tell you what's the significance. I'll definitely tell you what's the significance of his location. With pleasure, I'll tell you the significance of his location. The significance of his location is this. He's not in Ireland and this b – this young woman goes behind my back to him – behind my back, behind the back of someone senior to her – to inveigle him into doing her job for her. I would never describe any woman as manipulative and I did not, even under pressure. I acquainted him with the full story and I did let her know I was not impressed. Not impressed. This is not the way our company does its business, I told her. That was it, as far as interview panels were concerned for me. And you know, I was golfing recently with three men who took the package, one from the public service and the other two from financial services and they were telling me that they're busier than when they were working and that one of the things that keeps them busy is serving as a guest expert, I supposed you would call it, on interview panels in the civil service, the public service and private industry. Meanwhile I can't – well, I no longer see my way to – serve on interview panels in my own company. I ask you.

Quick as a flash I was asking him his goal for this coaching.

'If I am to be completely honest with you, I have been too busy to give it much consideration, so I wouldn't have a list of what I want from you. But I assume someone as experienced as yourself will offer me wonders…'

I restrained myself from telling him that to assume anything was to make an ass out of him and me. Instead, I said I'd study the transcript of his recording and it would provide the direction for our next session. He looked slightly crestfallen and made a neutral to negative noise about going along with whatever the expert recommended.

'Mary will have the transcript done by tomorrow afternoon,' I said. 'Would you like me to courier the DVD to you then, when we're done with it?'

His face lit up. Most people who undergo coaching want to take the DVDs away, mainly so they can stand on them immediately and put the shards into the wheelie bin. Some take them in order to watch their own progress from first day to last. A few take them because the coaching requires that they observe a particular pattern of communication happening. This man was taking his for entertainment. The appeal that has made Netflix profitable, only more local and personal. He wanted to watch himself talking.

'Who knows, I might learn something from it,' he said in a less than wholehearted salute to self-deprecation. 'Although my presentation skills – well, someone in the office once said I could talk for Europe.'

'Now, *there's* praise,' I said with a more than wholehearted salute to irony.

'Indeed,' he said. 'Indeed.'

Having seen him to the front door and watched him make his way towards Leeson Street Bridge, every ambassadorial inch of him, I leaned up against the glass until one of my colleagues asked if I was all right.

'Remember that cartoon you had on the wall of your office for a while? The one with the two vultures?'

She laughed and nodded.

'Sitting on the branch of a tree?'

'One of them's saying something to the other. Remind me?'

'It's saying, "Patience my ass, I'm gonna go kill somebody."'

'That's it. That sums up where I'm at, right now.'

'Unpleasant client?'

I shook my head. This man wasn't unpleasant. But so much was wrong with his self-presentation that I wasn't sure coaching would be of much value or of much immediate value to him. I looked at his CV again. He was fifty-six. And while I will fight ageism until the gerontological police come to get me, you don't see many people in their late fifties making radical changes in their lives. Especially when – as in this case – the fifty-six year old showed no evidence at all of a desire to change. Indeed (to use one of his own pet words) he evinced no interest in doing anything other than talking and – thereafter – watching himself talk.

Now, you might ask why I wasn't honest enough, during that first session, never mind later sessions, to call this man on his evident self-absorption and obsessive hogging of the conversational limelight. The wonderful David Maister wasn't talking about coaches when he addressed this problem but his observation applies:

'It is not enough for a professional to be *right*,' he said. 'An advisor's job is to be *helpful*. Proving to someone that they are wrong may be intellectually satisfying but it is not productive for either the client or the advisor.'

That's why I stayed silent during the session; because excoriating the man for his never-ending talk would not have been useful to either of us. (Except to the degree that getting something off your chest has a vicious satisfaction to it, no matter how much you subsequently regret it.)

While Mary was typing up the transcript, I went back to the emails setting up the coaching sessions. The man's PA had first telephoned, then sent through a numbered purchase order, indicating that their company was purchasing between two and four coaching sessions for their executive and reserving the option to purchase follow-up sessions as required. This didn't give the information on which I could decide whether this man had been instructed to undergo coaching or had chosen to come for coaching himself.

In theory, the latter is an enormous advantage, because the executive is prepared either to invest their own money or to request that their employer invests training money in them and a greater individual commitment inheres in such a decision. In practice, something was skewed. It didn't add up. At the end of the introductory couple of hours, I could not pin down what it was that might have led this man to autonomously choose to be coached.

When executives have coaching suggested to them by their boss or another senior figure in their company, that boss or senior figure will often contact the coach in advance to outline what should be addressed in the sessions. They will do this openly. It's not hidden from the person being coached.

As issues arise in coaching, either the person being coached will say, 'I'll go and check with X what's the answer to that,' or will indicate that they're happy for the coach to reach and question the referee. However, in this particular case, because the man had referred himself, I could not go back to his company in order to get clarification around the goals and objectives of which he seemed warmly to approve but of which he didn't seem to have any.

The moment the transcript came back, I sat down and began to work with it. Sometimes, when I believe the visual carries extra clues, I will keep the DVD for viewing and give it to the client at the next session. It is amazing how much you can learn from even the first forty-five seconds of an interview, especially if you play some of it back in slow motion.

In this case, however, the first *thirty* seconds of the transcript provided evidence of several problems. The first question would have been a version of 'What's the story?' It would have been an ostensibly casual query, inviting the man to share what it was he wanted to achieve out of the coaching: what problem he needed to solve, what discomfort he needed to address, what extra skill he needed to develop.

Here's the answer.

'Throughout my years as a manager, I've always held that a company's people are its greatest asset, so I would be positive when your name came up. Aside, of course, from the pleasure of telling my lovely wife that you are as glamorous in person as you are on the television. I would look forward to any tips and tricks you might give me that might improve my communication.'

Now, what does that answer tell us?

It tells us, first of all, that the man involved doesn't want to answer the simple and unthreatening question. He has the choice and he chooses to move into the past; to focus on his many years as a manager.

He could have one of two reasons for this evasion. The first and simplest is that he is a conscript. He has been volunteered, rather than volunteering, and he isn't happy about it. One way to remove himself from the discomfort of the present is to talk about the past.

Another reason could be that he's not a good listener and didn't actually hear the incoming question. This would have some support from the fact that the question was put to him again not once but, in different forms, a couple of times, and at no stage did he provide a straight answer or genuinely address the interrogative. However, he did hear other questions and did answer them without problem, so the betting favours him being an unwilling conscript engaging in avoidance behaviour.

The next phrase is just as telling.

'I've always held…'

Quoting yourself is a verbal indicator. Meaning that it

establishes much more than it intends to. The transmitter doesn't even register that they have done so. The receiver may not, either. The phrase floats past, masquerading as a meaningless filler, which it never is.

People who are young or modest never quote themselves. It is primarily a habit of chronological or attitudinal age. Meaning that you don't have to be really old to develop self-quotation as a habit. It can start as early as the forties. It should, of course, *never* start but when it does, some friend, colleague or relative should grasp the self-quoter warmly by the throat and warn him (or her, although so far it's a more male than female habit) not to do it again. Quoting oneself promotes one to a position of authority, assumes superiority over others and is intrinsically so self-regarding as to be toxic. Let's face it, if you choose your own quotations over those available from Einstein, Steve Jobs, Shakespeare, Roosevelt and Mark Twain, not to mention dozens of other verbose quote-generators, you're pretty likely to suffer from the kind of disproportionate self-regard which is just one notch short of referring to yourself in the third person.

Frequently, when people quote themselves, as in this particular case, they are in fact quoting general received wisdom without realising that it has been around for some time. The axiom that 'our people are our greatest asset' is a cliché favoured, these many decades, by politicians and captains of industry alike.

What's important about the use of such a concept is what it says about the user. What it says is that this person tends to interpret the obvious as being insightful and tends to find comfort in safe, largely meaningless bromides.

It can also be illustrative of another characteristic: the user may be self-absorbed but not self-observant; a variant on 'He may not think much of himself but he's all he ever thinks about.'

Still within the same sentence, we get, 'So I would be positive when your name came up.' Never mind the ropy syntax. In less than ten words, this man has revealed that he didn't choose to come for coaching. The oddity of the conditional future tense 'would be' meets the narrative clarity of 'when your name came up'. This is called 'truth leakage'. The man hasn't admitted that he's been told to come to me and throughout the rest of the briefing, he resolutely walks away from even the possibility of such a thing. But hanging in the statement is the possibility that when coaching was proposed, he could have taken a negative attitude, although this didn't happen.

In the course of an unthought-out introductory comment, this man goes on to make a ham-fisted attempt at a compliment, in the course of which he doesn't name his 'lovely' wife and tops it all off by insulting me: I might give him *tips and tricks*. The insult is unintended and irrelevant but if you look again at just that opening statement, what you can see, almost at a glance, is that here is a man who is not comfortable where he is and who is trying to wrap himself in his experience.

Now if you look at the second paragraph of this man's monologue, you can see that he's been asked the question as to why he's attending the session. This is the second time he's been asked it and a pattern of coping behaviour is emerging. When this man doesn't like a question because answering it honestly would require him to invade his own comfort zone and talk honestly about some aspect of himself about which he clearly doesn't want to talk, what he does is move into commentator mode. He's already commented on what he sees as the demonising of a number of bankers. Now he moves into defending Brian Cowen. Nobody had mentioned Brian Cowen, or commented either positively or negatively about the former Taoiseach.

As soon as he believes he has distracted from the discomfiting question (whereas what he has actually done is distract *himself*, rather than the questioner), he gets more confident and moves into mentor or lecturer mode, passing on wisdom he perceives himself as having. This is something that comes with seniority and should not. The provision of unsought advice always feels to the provider like a virtue but is often experienced by the recipient as a power play. It's a bit like swordplay in old movies. The actor who jumps on to a table is always going to win the sword fight because the person forced to look up and fight upward is at a disadvantage.

The person who gives advice, unasked, adopts the position of the table-based sword fighter: they are asserting their power or superiority over someone else.

The use of this particular bit of advice – 'to assume is to make an ass out of you and me'– is offensive for two other reasons. It's not just that the advice-giver is providing something the other person neither asked for nor wants. It's that the advice-giver is criticising the other person for the use of a simple and obvious word. And because it's the most godawful pointless old drivel. It pops up in the early pages of *The Silence of the Lambs*, where the FBI boss of Special Agent Clarice Starling quotes it to her. It isn't new to Clarice but she doesn't let on, because her boss is a decent man. *The Silence of the Lambs* was first published in 1989 – and even back then the 'assume' lecture was yawningly old.

It emerges that this man has a habit of offering unsought advice and that he characterises this as 'mentoring.' When he moves on to patronising the entire population of America and being racist about Italians, the reader begins to believe that although this man is only in his fifties, he is much older than his chronological age. He may have been a great manager in his day but the disrespectful diminution of staff in his department – 'One of the [nameless] little ones' makes that doubtful. The doubt is exacerbated by his narrative about involvement in recruitment interviews. Through his own words, the man reveals himself as:

Seeking to 'own' what is another executive's area of responsibility:
If anybody were to sit the members of the panel down for advance briefing/discussion, it should more properly have been the HR manager.

Having contempt for further education:
'This may be flavour of the month coming from someMBA course…'

Seriously bothered by something that happened more than six years ago:
He can remember the week and the month, never mind the year.

Suspicious and contemptuous of others:
He describes those who argue with him or oppose him as 'having an agenda', thereby devaluing what they say as deriving from some fell invidious illegitimate intent.

Sexist:
His outpouring about maternity leave has the flavour of a long-festering grievance. In addition, his insistence in the face of the HR director's advice on asking questions which would put him and the Barrisco corporation in court, sure as shooting, indicates more than that he is being old-fashioned.

Not in emotional control:
As this man explained his situation to me, he began to repeat phrases. This is a self-soothing device we learn as children. Hearing ourselves say the same phrase re-emphasises its truth to us. However, nobody who is in confident control of themselves needs verbal self-soothing.

What struck me, as I read the transcript, was the strength of the fear underlying his communication. Of course, this man might be one of those monologuists who never recognise an oncoming full stop at the best of times but – seen in print – his continuous transmission had the appearance of fending off awkward questions while defending against any possible negative perceptions I might have or develop about him. He wanted me to understand that he knew people who mattered, that he was a popular and influential leader. The evidence he adduced or in some cases failed to adduce pointed away, rather than towards, that conclusion.

This man's life-defining experiences were all in the past. He was at sea in the present and perceived key aspects of contemporary life, such as the (slow) rise of women into the ranks of management and the onward march of technology as requiring to be controlled or opposed by him. He was not a shareholder in Barrisco, a highly profitable company even during the recession, so whatever effect maternity leave had on its company line was a) provably manageable and b) impacted on him, personally, not at all. Yet he had vocalised his hostility to women in the workplace with such injudicious vehemence that the much younger – and female – Head of Human Resources had gone over his head to a corporate Vice-President in order to have him removed from an interview panel, which in turn greatly embittered him.

Making notes of what I would have to explore with him on the next visit, I went back through the transcript. His first – and final – conflict with the woman later promoted to be Vice-President in charge of human resources within Barrisco had happened in 2006, yet he had given that encounter more time and emotional temperature than almost anything that had happened in the ensuing seven years. Why was that? I wondered. The woman involved seemed to have been ruthlessly clear about getting him out of a process wherein she may have considered him to be a real and present danger because of his sense of entitlement to ask questions in the course of the interview which were neither appropriate, proper nor legal.

- Did she have to put her concerns in writing to someone in another country?
- Did she intend her email to have the impact it did?
- Did she fully understand how devastating a data-rich email can be, given the absence of tone, nuance, gesture or facial expression?
- Did her promotion to a much more important post in the corporation's HQ happen directly after this incident and was it consequent upon it – the man she had canned might feel doubly embittered if he believed she had profited from, as he saw it, informing on him.

One of the sentences in the final page of the transcript stood out in sharp relief. Where my client was describing the HR manager selling him down the river to a higher boss, he talked of telling the VP in Tobago 'the full story'. He also told the HR woman he was not impressed by her. But apart from enabling him to express his feelings, neither input appeared to have had any outcome. He was still, it would seem, removed from the interview panel and never subsequently served on one, which would be unusual in such a company. The woman involved, on the other hand, had been promoted, which calls into question the declaration he made to her in the middle of their row: 'That is not the way our company does its business.'

The only thing that was inescapably clear from study of the transcript is that this was a man under enormous personal and career pressure. Some third party appeared to have recommended my company's coaching to him. Or instructed him to attend.

I walked around this man's situation in my head often in the following few days. As a coach, it's my job to help someone firstly understand and secondly improve their situation, if they want to improve it. Pivotal to me being helpful to any client is getting their capacity right:

- Their capacity to look in a fresh way at their life and career
- Their capacity to analyse what's happening to them and work out how much they can control or influence it
- Their capacity to understand and accept what I might say to them
- And finally, their capacity to change

Whether in training or in coaching, one of the central rules we apply is that you never alert a client to a problem they can't solve. If, for example, someone is incapable of critical thinking, telling them they have a deficit in that area does nothing to improve their situation but can, instead, add to their difficulties. Applying that rule to this man's situation meant that most of what I had observed and what I've outlined here on earlier pages could not be usefully presented to him. To take just one example, it would not develop his performance to tell him that his self-presentation was of a bigoted male chauvinist and that he was lucky not to have found himself in court over some of what he had articulated on the topic of women in the workplace. The HR executive, back in 2006, had tried to educate him about how the methods of job interviewing had developed and this hadn't led to him developing his skills. It would be dangerous to assume I could be any better, as a catalyst, than she had been. Even though it was possible that the two personalities had been incompatible, the rest of what the man had told me argued that he was not going to change his views, no matter what kind of personality was to work with him on them.

Not that he, or anybody else, would be employed for their views. Your views are your own business. What your employer buys is your *actions*. The difference is that you can be the most resentful human in the world. You may believe yourself to be an under-appreciated Einstein and privately long for the day when the company employing you goes bankrupt. But as long as your behaviour doesn't match your views, everything's dandy. People buy behaviour, not underlying attitude.

The problem is that, to use that great current management word, behaviour and attitude tend to be *aligned*. I do have a friend, whose mindset is all Eastern mysticism and semi-starvation, who manages every few years to disappear to Nepal for six months but who at all other times is a suited and booted officer in a multinational company. But he's a rare, rare individual. His capacity to hold one set of attitudes while aligning (there's that word again) his quotidian behaviour with a quite different set of values is unusual. The man who could talk for Europe was unlikely to have that rare capacity, as evidenced by the amount of inadvertent truth-leakage in his introductory session with me. The chances of him learning to behave in all the ways that demonstrate gender equality at all times in his place of work? Somewhere between slim and none.

So it was that I welcomed him back with some confusion. I didn't want to irritate him by going back to the goals and objectives bit but the warning frequently deployed by my husband was ringing in my head: 'If you have no port to go to, you're favoured by no wind.'

Within minutes, my husband was proved right. Yet again. We didn't have a shortage of wind. But it blew in random, whimsical directions. Not uninteresting, some of them.

We covered – sorry, *he* covered how irritating it was to have newspapers constantly moaning about losing money and market share to social media while at the same time putting internet links in the middle or at the end of stories in their print edition. He covered the over-sensitivity of the dashboard icons in BMWs and his theory that their constant lighting up was a marketing device, manipulative in intent, designed to get you back to the garage even though nothing was really wrong with the car. He covered the willingness of business people who claimed to be good Catholics to nonetheless get items manufactured in China without making any real effort to assess the work environment where the items were made as to its potential to cause or contribute to worker suicides. He covered the changes at the top of his own corporation and opined that shifts and promotions in Nebraska would have relatively little effect in Ireland, because the Irish plan was solidly profitable and anyway, the 10 per cent tax rate in this country ensured US attitudes to the Irish operation were as warm and soft as a lagging jacket. (OK, the lagging jacket is my analogy. I did a lot of mental illustration and doodling while I listened.)

With ten minutes to go, I decided to make one more stab at locating a port, as in some kind of objective that would direct this man's capacity to talk into some channel that might be productive for him.

'What does your wife think of where you're at, right now?'

If I was a SWAT team and had thrown a flashbang into a small dark room, it couldn't have had a greater effect. Or effects. He went silent. He sat still as a statue. So did I. I had no idea which vein I'd hit or why, but blithering into the silence was severely contra-indicated. My internal stop-watch clunked into action, telling me when thirty seconds had elapsed, then forty-five, then a minute.

'She says take the package.'

'What package?'

'The early retirement package.'

'Why?'

'Because it's – because she says – just take it.'

'You know what?' I said. 'We should in theory be coming to the end of this session but I had a cancellation this morning and I could work on if you could.'

He nodded, silently. I doubt if he knew what time it was or was even that sure whether it was morning or afternoon. I alerted him to the location of the nearest Gents and went off to ask someone to bring us fresh coffee. Serving him, I thought he might wear a circular hole in the bottom of the cup, he stirred it so long after putting the sugar in it. Eventually, he looked at me, waiting for another question.

'How did a retirement package come into play?'

His area of the business was shrinking in importance and while of course he had options to head up other areas of the business, the possibility had been raised that he might prefer to look at the external options offered by an early severance package. That was the official version he presented. As he talked, the unofficial version began to seep through: Here's your hat, what's your hurry? At his most recent appraisal, he had been offered counselling with me as a way of preparing him for departure. That, in itself, was odd. I don't do counselling and nowhere on the website of The Communications Clinic will you find the smallest reference to counselling. No great benefit to him would have emerged from poking around in the area but I wondered if he had chosen us and reinterpreted 'coaching' as 'counselling'. Perhaps 'coaching' carried the implication of preparing for a more positive future.

I had to concentrate hard. This man might – indeed, did – talk a great deal but his manner of communication could best be likened to make-believe mahogany: a thin strip of the real thing overlaid on chipboard to give the impression of solid hard wood. What he said was the thin strip of real mahogany. What he meant was the chipboard. He was scrupulously truthful but had something of a genius for selectivity and post-factum reinterpretation, so if you didn't keep your wits about you, the impression you ended up with matched the facts only occasionally and at random. In the case of his briefing on this particular day, the impression a casual listener would get was that of a man not even close to retirement age who had seen major possibilities in the wider commercial world for his multifaceted talents and experience and had done a clever deal with his current employer which had netted him a severance package that would start immediately, thus effectively giving him a salary for the years up to official retirement age. In addition, this interpretation suggested, he had persuaded his employer to commission The Communications Clinic and specifically me to work with him on exploring options so that he ended up in some role appropriate to the final years of a stellar career.

Underneath all this, the chipboard reality carried a lumpier truth. The company had decided that a man who might have been productive in his earlier years was no longer productive. They had further decided that someone taking so little cognisance of the laws related to equality and bullying might be a corporate risk that training programmes were not going to make less risky. The scale of the severance package being hinted at was an indicator of the decency of a company which, when it couldn't solve a problem, threw money at it and the cover of coaching over it. Not the worst combination and fairly respectful of them that they hadn't come around to the back door to tell me what I should and shouldn't do for their soon-to-be ex employee. They left the man his dignity and his coaching privacy.

The second session was mainly devoted to allowing him to recover himself, after the question about his wife, by talking. Talking seemed to be the equivalent of burn ointment for this man's scorched feelings. As long as he kept talking, talking, talking, it seemed to sooth and distract him from the humiliating experience he was going through.

During the third session, I tried to get him to concentrate on what he was going to do after the date of his parting. He planned, he said, to apply for CEO posts in prestigious organisations. Fine. Which ones? The list became very small as he realised that, whether because of relative inexperience or different ethos or unacceptable location, one after another would be less than perfect.

Then he moved on to directorships, making a list of his golfing and other friends who owned companies or sat on the boards of plcs. I privately thought this might be a relatively easy option, to the extent that men who had stayed friends with this man despite the relentlessness of his verbal flow were unlikely to be deterred by said flow on the board of a company. This would not apply to a woman of matching verbosity but then places on boards are shockingly difficult for women to access, despite the passage of time. Men on boards like to be with their own and whatever else this man was, he was a golf-playing, lizard-wearing man's man.

By the time we parted, two sessions later, he was already gone from the company, after a presentation at which people said all the right things and none of the wrong things and he himself talked for thirty-five minutes. The irritation value of him speaking for that duration would, one imagines, have been counterweighted in the minds of the listeners by the glad prospect of it being the last time they would ever, jointly or severally, have to listen to him.

His wife had arranged to borrow a friend's house in Fort Lauderdale for seven weeks, which seemed just about the right length of time to create a buffer between his past and his present. A charity had invited him to go on their board, an invitation accepted with alacrity. Thanks to his wife, who seemed to be a rock of sense, and to his company, which operated a ruthless but generous form of capitalism, he faced a comfortable retirement at an age when he could enjoy it – an age when many of the recession-struck were unwillingly facing almost twenty years more before they could begin to think of hanging up their work boots.

CAREER PITFALL #6: FAILURE TO CHANGE WITH THE TIMES

Were this chapter to come with a health warning, that health warning would read: *You don't need to be old to be a talkative inflexible chauvinist.*

Talking too much starts early and is often taken as a good, rather than a bad executive trait. The problem with being a talker is that it can take up all available cognitive space, blocking important incoming messages. Allied to contempt for the new, it can become a real problem.

Contempt for the new is a constant in people beyond a certain age but *expressed* contempt for the new is rare, largely because the older generation knows that they minute they say, 'Twitter is a waste of time,' or, 'I don't know how anybody gets through the day without first sitting down and reading the newspaper,' or, 'Young people today spend their whole time on Facebook' they will be assumed to be old as a Georgian building and not amenable to a refurb.

To be a neophiliac (as opposed to a neophobe) has its down-sides. The homes of neophiliacs are filled with once *avant-garde* gadgets and clothing and their PCs are clogged with software (remember BEBO? MySpace?) that never caught on or caught on only briefly. Neophiliac companies tend to flatter themselves that they're 'learning organisations', while buying whatever training programmes are fashionable at the time. Generalised talk-shop diversity training had a vogue until companies realised it created more problems than it solved.

Bottom line? Find a way to explore the new. Every day. Every week. Particularly new employment law. It doesn't matter if you believe that, say, Ireland's bullying laws are weird. The law is still the law and must be obeyed. Establishing your individuality by breaking the rules and explaining to the rule-makers how mistaken they were is a guaranteed path to career failure.

Five Tips for You as Your Own Coach

1. Ask someone close to you to be your bad habit monitor. They're to tell you if you're swearing, telling the same story over and over, interrupting people or just talking too much, even if it's not about yourself. You agree to hear their observations and not to hold it against them.

2. Learn at least five computer or smartphone shortcuts a week.

3. Learn from the opposite sex. If you're male, learn that women don't go for the 'I'll take ya' knock-down, drag-out row approach to resolving a difference of view. If you're female, get a bit more upfront in challenging inappropriate behaviour without making a great time-consuming issue out of it.

4. Find other people interesting and ask questions so you learn from each and every one you encounter in the course of your working day.

5. Shut up. Lyndon Johnson had a sign on his wall that read: 'YOU AIN'T LEARNING NOTHIN' WHEN YOU'RE DOIN' ALL THE TALKIN.'

   It's just amazing what you hear when you're not talking. However, of just as much if not greater importance is the fact that some talk addicts lose the capacity to moderate their output. They can do complete silence, the way a binge drinker can get through a couple of days on 7Up, but they can't do moderation and they deceive themselves constantly about how much they contribute in any human encounter. Oliver St John Gogarty captured the issue in a tiny vignette about a barrister friend of his, who went to condole with the widow of one of Ireland's presidents.

   'He spoke for an hour without a break and without giving her a chance even of a sigh,' wrote Gogarty, 'and then, coming out, remarked, "A nice chatty little woman."'

7

The Dead-Catter

Suzanne arrived on a Monday morning. Not just any Monday morning. The Monday morning after the summer rain. The summer being 2013, which, up to that downpour, had been so dry, gorse fires were breaking out on Howth to enliven the days of those living up the hill. It wasn't that much of a downpour, either, but dried-out soil absorbs rain poorly, sending it instead to drainpipes clogged with dried leaves, causing backups and flash floods in the least expected locations. Letterkenny General Hospital was one of those locations. The Old Synagogue in Dublin was another. This surprised the hell out of us.

Over that weekend, we were bothered by our inability to get on the internet from home. We were even more bothered when, after the weekend, having come to work in the office, we *still* couldn't get on. It was at this point, around eight in the morning, that someone went to have a look at the server and found it, in the basement, up to its electronic knees in water. Which sodden state would explain its unwillingness to tap-dance as per normal. It also meant that the entire basement of our new premises (new in the sense of us moving into it) was flooded to a depth of several inches, which did nothing for the new carpet and created a vague but pronounced stench that rose slowly but confidently through the building.

I poured dry coffee grounds into saucepans and frying pans and put them on the hob to scorch. It's an old trick from the wagon-train days that's supposed to remove the worst pong. Or at least present the olfactories with a marginally better alternative. Other staff members set off to buy Febreze. And we put incoming clients into rooms as near the roof of our building as possible.

One of those clients was Suzanne Greene, who, according to the executive who brought her to the room where I was to work with her, had concerns about confidentiality. What concerns would they be, I asked him.

'I don't exactly know,' he said.

'Well, how did they manifest themselves?'

He blinked, trying to work out how he'd got himself into this mess.

'I said, "Hi, Suzanne, you're here for a coaching session with Terry?"' he said. 'And she said, "Yes," and I said I'd bring her to the Elliman room and I offered her coffee and tea and she wanted to know how I knew she was here for coaching?'

Ms Greene had seemed very bothered that someone other than me knew what she was in for, or maybe that she was with us at all. I checked and double-checked – had anything else been said? Nothing. I took a folder and headed for the room where we were due to work. She was standing just inside the door of the room, clutching her bag as if ready for departure.

'Leaving that quickly?' I said, extending a hand.

She gave me a limp handshake and said no, she just didn't know where to sit. That surprised me. Where to sit is a choice for most people, rather than a challenge. You'll have groups who automatically line up on one side of a table and then make jokes, as others sit on the other side of it, that it's all very conflictual. You'll have people who automatically leave the place at the head of the table empty because they expect the trainer or coach to take that position, whereas others will leave a seat half-way down one side, because whatever training courses they've already attended put the trainer in the middle, rather than at the top.

I did a big vague gesture and very decidedly sat down on one side of the long oval.

'Where do you want me to sit?' she asked, as if the gesture had not happened.

'Wherever you wish.'

That seemed to vex her but she sat down opposite me, her handbag at the side of her right leg. In front of her was a glass of water.

'You're sure you wouldn't like coffee or tea?'

She shook her head. According to her CV she was forty-one but she looked older. Or perhaps not older but faded. Her hair and skin colour had a powdered look to them, as if she worked with chalk. She wore neither rings nor nail varnish and clutched the first three fingers of her left hand with the first three fingers of her right hand.

'Who was the man who put me – who brought me here?'

'Why?'

She looked astonished and affronted.

'*Why?*'

I smiled at her.

'Did he charm you so much you'd prefer to work with him?'

'No.'

I sat quietly.

'So you won't tell me his name? It doesn't matter to you how worried I am about confidentiality?'

'How does his name affect our confidentiality?'

'He knew I was here to be coached by you.'

'He did.'

'Why did he know that?'

'So that he could bring you to the right room.'

'But how did he know it was coaching?'

'We have codes which go in the calendar.'

'Who sees your calendar?'

'Our staff.'

'All your staff?'

'We don't have a cast of thousands. Yet.'

'So *all* your staff could see what I was here for?'

'The codes are just so effective. TG means training, so they must get one of the rooms with training equipment in it. PR means what it sounds like, so no need for recording. C means it's a one-to-one coaching session, which means a cosy smaller room.'

'Why would all your staff have access to my appointment?'

'If our PR people have a meeting, if Eoghan has a training course upstairs and Hilary one downstairs, if Stephanie is organising coffee and biscuits and HaiYing is on the phones, then one of our other executives will answer the door and when they welcome someone like yourself, it's better if they have some sense of who you're seeing and why.'

'I would have severe reservations about that. This isn't just a data protection issue, it is a privacy issue.'

'Are you here to be coached out of paranoia?'

'I *beg* your pardon? What did you say?'

'No, no. You heard me.'

'You're accusing me of paranoia?'

'Stating, rather than accusing. It's legal to be paranoid.'

'Why would I be paranoid?'

'Dunno. You being blackmailed?'

'Of course not. What do you think I am?'

A spectacularly suspicious, cold and hostile pain in the arse was the honest answer but I did a shoulder shrug, rather than articulate it. If this woman was as paranoid as she seemed, to the extent that she might be tipping into mental illness, the immediate truth was not likely to be helpful to her. On the other hand, going any further down the road we were currently on wasn't going to solve her problems either. She kept switching hands, doing the three-finger clutch on one, then the other. The temptation to tell her to relax was prevented by sudden recall of thriller-writer Thomas McGuane's great observation that 'Telling people to relax is not as aggressive as shooting them but it's up there.' Not that I could have got the relax word in edgeways, anyway. She was on a mission, was this client.

'Why did you suggest I was being blackmailed? What do you think I would be blackmailed about?'

'Haven't given it a thought. Didn't suggest anything. Blackmail came up in my mind because sometimes we don't put names or codes on the calendar at all, if the reason the client is coming to us is extremely sensitive. We do work in relation to court cases. And we've dealt with clients who have been stalked or blackmailed and, in that situation, only me and Stephanie would ever know anything about it.' I looked at my watch. 'Suzanne, you're fifteen minutes into your hour. You can go now and we won't charge you anything and we'll excise you from our records as if you never existed, or you can get on with whatever you wanted to achieve by coming here.'

'Well, that's not what I would have expected but maybe – I suppose I should have realised that you're just in the business of making money.'

'What did you think I was in the business of?' I asked the question very gently because otherwise I would have been on my feet ordering her the hell out of our building.

'Not giving ultimatums, anyway.'

'Well, there you are,' I said and stood up.

'So now I'm being thrown out, is that it?'

'No, I'm going to leave you here to decide what you want to do. I'll get Steph to drop in on you in about five minutes.'

'I don't want anybody else in on – I don't want that. I want what I came for.'

Down I sat again.

'What did you come for?'

'You can't just shift me away from my concerns like that. And you needn't tell me I have so much time left. I've never failed to pay a bill in my life.'

She then got herself up a conversational cul-de-sac, admitting that she wasn't paying for this session anyway, that her company, an accountancy partnership, was paying.

'Why?'

'Because I questioned a process. I said, and I indicated that I might take this further, that someone – I won't name him – had an agenda and I wouldn't take immediate action but it was definitely, I didn't say rigged, I'm not that stupid and I have more self-control, but they could work it out. And they said they would pay for this and I asked what they hoped to force me into and they said it was part of a process that before they addressed contentious issues they didn't go first to the bit about offering remedial training because at my level that would not be apposite because I wouldn't have got to my present position in the firm if I did not have the full suite of necessary skills so it would be – they didn't say it but I knew what they meant if they never said it – it would be insulting and actionable if they put me on a training course, ridiculous, so they have come up with something that would look good when it ends up in court – that's what my brother said when I asked him about the coaching, he's a solicitor and he said it would do no harm to turn up for the first session anyway, because – never mind.'

She shut down so unexpectedly that I found myself slightly dazed. Her solicitor brother had told her to make a token appearance in my office at least once, presumably because it would look better later if her company made her redundant or fired her with cause? Or perhaps it was just to force her company to pay cash for something she never planned to make real use of?

'Anyway, I'm here now,' she summarised.

'Let's see if I've understood…You went for a promotion? You're an accountant?'

She shook her head. She had a commerce degree but was not an accountant. She worked in administration and had gone for promotion from Grade 3 to Grade 2. The interview had been a patent set-up and the other person had been appointed so quickly thereafter, anybody could see the whole thing was a ready-up and she didn't mind telling me she had stated that without fear or favour and it had not gone down well with the management. As far as I could make out, Suzanne Greene had been passed over for promotion by someone younger, although only five years younger, who had no academic advantages over her. It was not gender discrimination, she was quick to accept; the person promoted was female.

'So why do you think they picked her, rather than you?'

It was a matter of culture, she said. The culture of the firm favoured yes men. If you didn't immediately agree with everything you were marked out and excluded. But she had never been willing to accept that kind of thing and – well – this was the end result. She wouldn't say it was typical because she had never gone for promotion before but what else would you expect of a firm where twelve out of the fifteen partners were men?

'Now, we're coming to the end of our time, today,' I started to say.

'That seems very short,' Ms Greene snapped.

'And what I'd like to do in our last five minutes is work out some plan so that we've something to aim at and we'll know when we've hit it. How many sessions are you expecting to attend?'

The company, she said, suggested three, but were prepared to pay for up to seven.

'Have they outlined any objectives, or agreed any goals with you?'

'They believe coaching would help me align my objectives with the values of the partnership and establish clarity to the satis-faction of both parties.'

'Both parties being you and them?'

She nodded and went on to say that the letter she had received from HR said that they would provide the coach with a background briefing if she found this acceptable but she didn't. How could it be acceptable for someone outside the company to be briefed by Personnel about the – about the private issues of an employee? How could this be done without being in breach of every data protection law in the land?

I left the rhetorical questions to fester where they fell.

'So they won't ring me and I won't ring them?'

'Under no circumstances.'

That was a no, then.

'OK, you'll set up the next meeting and we'll take it from there.'

One week later, she was giving me her background details. She was the middle of three female siblings born close to each other to two librarians and had one brother ten years younger than her (the solicitor). Said librarians now living in Florida. Her older sister worked in publishing, her younger was a nurse. When I asked her if they were close, as a family, she asked for a definition of 'close', in itself an answer. She lived on her own in an apartment in the IFSC and although she knew how to drive, chose to use public transport and walk.

She had been with her present employer for eleven years, having worked for three other companies for shorter periods.

'What do you like about the company?'

'*Like* about it?'

She seemed genuinely fazed by the question, as if liking any aspect of an employing company was a stretch. After long thought, she said it wasn't something she thought about that much. It wasn't a ground-breaking company. In the early days of her career, she had hoped to work for a brilliant creative person like Steve Jobs or Jeff Bezos but it had never happened. The company she was now with was OK, she supposed. Except for her direct boss, who had an agenda and had pulled the wool over the eyes of all the other top management.

'What, precisely, is this man's agenda?'

'Oh, he *says* his duty, his first duty to the shareholder is to deliver profit.'

'As opposed to?'

'Once you start with profit, everything else gets swept aside. Nobody matters to the profit-making brigade. They'll pretend to listen but they don't, really. They put just enough perks in place to placate the masses and then they drive towards profit. And the majority of the workforce just go along, because it's easier and since the economic melt-down, they don't believe they have any choices. They're always on about negative equity and how this company is only operating three day weeks and how they dread the bills for their kids and can't afford to change their car.'

Riffling through my earlier notes, I saw that her employing company had thirty-five staff. Not exactly 'the masses', as I would have seen them, but Ms Green had moved on to point out that the company had in fact made no profits the previous year and the MD was under pressure, he said, from his board, to get it right this year and he was going around looking for credit for not reducing working hours or laying people off.

'Like we should be grateful,' she said, contemptuously. 'Even though he's still living in his big house in Stillorgan with the pillars. Of course he lets everybody know that it's worth about a third of what he paid for it six years ago so he can't get it sold and is stuck with it. Stuck with a nineteenth century house with servants' quarters. Why should I feel sorry for him? People should live within their means and cut their cloth according to their measure. I have only a tiny mortgage on my apartment.'

'How did you manage that?'

'What do you mean, how did I manage that?'

'Suzanne, repeating an awkward question may solve problems

for you in a busy workplace but it's a device we're all wise to, here. Just answer it, OK?'

'What kind of a statement – that suggests I deliberately avoid answering questions where I work – I find that objectionable.'

'Noted,' I said.

'I had a settlement and I pumped it all into paying off as much of the mortgage as possible.'

'Very sensible. A settlement of what?'

'The amount or the – the source?'

'The source.'

'Redundancy.'

'Oh?'

'That's another story.'

'Do tell.'

She had worked for a much larger company for four years and then, at her appraisal, they said they were embarking on a complete review and her section was going to be subsumed into another and so they could offer her redundancy and a very good reference. The redundancy amounted to three years' salary.

'They offered you no other options? Like deployment to another plant?'

She shook her head. I went back to the CV. The company involved was a reputable multinational. Something didn't add up but now was not the time to try to make the sums come out right.

'Go back to your current boss and his determination to make profit this year. How does this affect you and your area?'

'Well, I just explained to him that you can't just waltz in and demand 10 per cent more productivity. That's not going to happen. Saying it must happen and that it's a given won't change realities. Or presenting surveys.'

'Surveys?'

'Reports from other branches of the company where they've turned everything upside down, according to themselves, if you could believe them and produced more – all this stuff about working smarter. And quoting the new "intake"' – she sketched quotation marks in the air – 'coming up with bright ideas that some of us came up with years ago and had ignored but of course now it suits him to be presenting himself as Mr Innovation, Mr Forward Thinking to all these young ones straight out of college wet behind the ears know everything no respect for anything they didn't invent. Majority women and dressed as might be appropriate for a disco but they're not stupid, it gets them attention.'

'Maybe you'd give me an example of an idea you offered them ages ago and didn't have taken up but that has been taken up, coming from one of the new intake?'

She couldn't remember, there were so many. It had taken her a long time to realise that her boss – the founder of the company – was all talk, all image, all seeing himself in the business pages of *The Irish Times*. But no action based on what employees suggested to him. Her hands came up, palms facing me, as she made the point that the boss liked everybody to act happy clappy and be *positive*. Didn't want to know anything that wasn't *positive*. When she kept pointing out health and safety threats, including the platform shoes with five inch heels some of the younger ones were wearing, he told her not to worry about it and when – as was her duty, she told me – she had persisted and even put it in writing, had instituted what he called a consultative process which was just a way of letting the reckless outweigh her considered position and then he said that she had finished her stint on the health and safety committee, even though, up to then, nobody had ever heard of stints, it had been a permanent appointment, more or less.

'I've pointed out to him again and again that he's storing up trouble for himself and for the company by going soft on the new intake. Not a week goes by that I don't present him with a concrete example, sometimes in writing, so if he wanted to action it, he could immediately but all he does is sigh and thank me and he always has a meeting to go to or an urgent phone call to make to North Carolina so he's sorry but he has to cut me short although I can rest assured that he's registered the relative importance of what I have had to say to him.'

'Hold it. Say that last bit again?'

'He says I can rest assured that he's registered the relative importance of what I have had to say to him.'

'That's what he actually says? Those words?'

'Yes.'

'Every time?'

A silence fell. Funny how ever-present street noises swell into a conversational lull; ambulances whinged in the distance and two men talked animatedly in some Hispanic language directly outside the office.

'Do you not find it draughty in here?' Suzanne asked, shivering into the cardigan she had thrown over her shoulders. I apologised and shut the single long window that had been open, reflecting that at least its closure would prevent ingress of wasps, which, at the turn between August and September, were everywhere.

'Let's go back to your objectives – what you wish yourself to achieve during these coaching sessions,' I said. 'You talked – you said something about aligning yourself with something. In practical terms, what does that mean?'

'I agreed to come here and they seem to think you'll be able to – that what you offer could be of – of – could contribute to the enhancement of career-building relationship skills – career-building skills in my portfolio.'

'Who would you be close to, in the office?'

'Close to? How do you mean, close to? I have perfectly civil, perfectly functional relationships with everybody in the office and throughout the plant. What are you implying?'

'No implication in a positive question.'

'Perfectly good relationships. Working relationships. It would, of course, be easier if the management wasn't constantly shifting the goal posts and demanding – setting out different priorities. But fine. The man who recruited me is in North Carolina now but I would never presume on his recruiting me. You don't presume.'

'Who are you close to, outside the office?'

'Do you mean am I married because I'm not.'

'No, I knew that.'

She managed to bridle and look terrified at the same time and demanded to know why I would have believed it was my business to discuss her marital status with anybody? I flicked back the first two pages of her printed-out CV and turned the page thus revealed to her. Marital status, it said, single.

I watched with interest as a tide of red flowed up from the frilly neckline of her sweater through the matt make-up on her face to her hairline. She stiffly apologised and I flipped both hands to indicate that it was of no moment whatever. I could see her working backwards to locate the question she had misunderstood.

'I have three friends from school and we would go away together for weekends. Two of them are married, the third is divorced. I'm in a book club but I wouldn't be personally friendly with any of the members.'

'Do you talk about work to any of these people?'

'*No*. You don't cross boundaries.'

'So who do you talk about work to?'

Nobody, was the answer. I thanked her and let her out into the cooling autumn afternoon. When I was tidying the table we'd been at, I noticed that she had eaten a Kit-Kat from the piled plate. The strip of red paper from the outside of the biscuit/bar was neatly folded up, the silver foil rolled into so tightly compacted a ball, it could have served as a bullet.

When Suzanne returned a week later, she was in full battle-dress. Literally and metaphorically. Literally, she was wearing a sage-green safari suit in wild silk, the sleeves rolled to the elbow and captured by one of those buttoned flaps. Metaphorically, she had a crow to pluck. A very dead, very stinky crow, it seemed. She was tired of all this nonsense. She would have expected – indeed, *any reasonable person would have the right to expect* – that something would have come of all this chat, what else would she be wasting her time coming here week after week for otherwise? It was time, she announced, to stop all this 'what are you having yourself?' questioning and come to a conclusion. This was all said through almost gritted teeth and her hands had gone back to the three finger grip. When she finished, I poured coffee (don't usually do the pouring, because I'm likely to scald clients and we don't have enough of them to be casually hospitalising any).

'So what conclusions have you come to?' I asked, pushing the milk jug towards her.

'It isn't my job to come to conclusions. You're the coach. Supposedly.'

'Why do you say "supposedly"?'

'Well, to be honest with you – I'm sorry but I believe in telling it like it is – I haven't seen anything that I would count as coaching. Anybody can ask questions and just nod and look encouraging.'

'One of the problems of staying alive in this country at the moment is that almost nobody asks questions and nods and looks encouraging,' I said.

'You're well paid to do it.'

I looked at her attentively.

'Well, you are, I mean.'

One of the things you notice when you do a lot of coaching is that there comes a time in some of the more difficult encounters where the client demonstrates an almost suicidal desire to provoke the coach. Suzanne Greene had been circling that point for a while. Now she wanted to get to it more directly.

'This is just ridiculous, to be honest with you, it really is. I have gained nothing, because you haven't said anything. I could talk to the walls at home and get as much. I have a duty of care to my employer, too, and I must ensure that they get sufficient value out of this – this – *caper*. Not any more of this softly, softly, catchee monkey stuff.'

She was now one decibel shy of yelling at me and I'm weighing up telling her I won't be dictated to by her into doing her a disservice.

'Put it this way, it should be simple enough,' she continued. 'You can work out what – how you would react if I was working with you. Or for you. If that was the case how would you handle me?'

'If I was working with you I'd ask for a transfer. If you were working for me, I'd fire you.'

She stared at me.

'I'd have gone through all of the proper procedures to allow you the chance to change, to grow, to develop but if you insisted on staying the way you are, I would want you gone.'

I said it as quietly as I could, so she wouldn't be able to feed off any energy that anger might give what I was saying.

'Why?'

'Because you're the most negative person I've ever encountered. As a coach, I'll happily work with you to fix that if you want to, but if I was a colleague of yours, it'd be like the advice they give on aeroplanes. You know when they say to put the oxygen mask on your own face first, before going to help anyone else travelling with you? That's because you could lose consciousness while trying to get the mask on a child and then the child wouldn't be able to help *you*. If I worked with you, self-preservation would come into play.'

She immediately accused me of having talked to her boss. I shook my head.

'Well, *communicated* with him.'

I listed the possibilities off on my fingers; 'Talk to him? No.

Email him? No. Fax? No. Text? No. Not directly, not indirectly. Not taking the initiative. Not passively. I have never shared the smallest bit of information with your boss at any point. Go check with him, he'll confirm it.'

'He once quoted you to me.'

I started to say that he couldn't have and then realised that of course he could quote something I'd said that someone else had passed on or that he'd read in one of my books.

'He said you would say I was 'dead-catting''.'

'Oh, arriving in to him all the time with some problem for him to solve?'

'Which is what middle management within any organisation is supposed to do.'

'Nope. Middle management can solve a lot of problems without carrying them around like dead cats to toss on someone else's desk. And even if they haven't the authority to solve the problem on their own initiative, they should always arrive at the office of the person to whom they report with at least a suggested solution.'

'He's a nice man, really,' she said. It was a kind of surrender. She got up and walked around the room, I suspect because it meant she had to look at me less, that way. She asked me, if her boss and I both thought her so toxic, how she had got that way. I said I didn't know and I didn't care, that she could get into psychoanalysis on her own time but that a more urgent task, if she was to survive the world of work, was to change the behaviour, rather than going deep-sea diving, in psychological terms, to identify the causative factors.

'Oh, the usual stuff,' she said and for the first time outside a bad historical novel, I saw a lip curl. 'Use affirmative language and body language.'

It had the sound of a quotation, so I asked where the dictum had come from. Her boss had said it to her some time previously when someone had complained. Yes, she said, in answer to the unasked question, several of her colleagues had contributed to her miseries, in the past year, one of them choosing to close down a staff meeting with astonishing and very obvious abruptness before going directly to her boss to complain that she was impossible at meetings. She sat down again and put her head in her hands, then ran her hands up over her forehead and through her hair.

'He said and I quote, because I was there and I made notes in case of litigation, "that bitch has never seen an idea she didn't want to fucking crush, never seen a happy human she didn't want to depress, never come to any staff meeting without the intention to poison and destroy and either she fucking goes or I do." Knowing, of course, that as the highest producing marketing executive in the business and a pal from their days in Gonzaga of the boss, not to mention being shareholder, there was never going to be a choice between us.'

That said, she admitted that the boss had ticked his friend off for what he had said and brought in a facilitator to mediate between his two staff. The mediator had established that Suzanne wouldn't sue the man who had called her a bitch, or trigger a bullying case against him, and he would ensure that a detailed report of every meeting would be emailed to her directly after it happened, so she could input in writing if she wanted to, although she never had, in the ensuing three months.

By this stage, we were running out of time, so it wasn't until a week later that we got to meet again. The interval allowed me to go back over my notes and to have a think about Suzanne's situation. Her boss seemed to be a tolerant, kind and supportive man, who had gone to the trouble to read material about toxic and negative people before presenting alternatives to his problem employee. Little doubt seemed to hang around the likelihood of Suzanne being a problem employee and it would be a bet on a certainty that the previous employer who had provided her with a generous package and a good reference had also found her impossible and had come up with a fur-lined exit chute.

Because of the way employment law is structured, the volatile executive who had sworn at her and thrown down ultimata to the effect that it was him or her stood gravely endangered by his own behaviour, with which any reasonable human being would sympathise. But the fact that every reasonable human being might sympathise does not bring the law on to his side and it assuredly was not on his side. Never mind to what degree Suzanne had contributed to her own downfall, no executive can be permitted to behave as this man had.

Here again, her boss had evidently tried to be fair-minded and equitable, seeking to deliver justice to his former schoolmate while vindicating Suzanne's interests by bringing in a facilitator. While the sequence that had led to her being sent to me for coaching wasn't as clear and I didn't plan to probe it for fear that revealing how it had happened would humiliate or upset her, it was obvious that this coaching was Last Chance Saloon: that if Suzanne could not turn around her behaviour in response to working with me, her company would get rid of her, sooner or later. In one sense, talking with Damien, her thoughtful boss, might have been helpful to make sure I wasn't barking up the wrong tree but as barking and trees went, this was pretty well guaranteed to be the correct tree, so it didn't matter that I couldn't talk to him directly. It might help to know if he regarded the coaching as a final gift to a departing employee or as a final effort to improve her performance in her present job but we were going to have to manage without this information.

When she arrived, the next day, I asked her what she'd been thinking about since the last session. She sat slumped in the chair in the suit she'd worn to our first encounter and did that sigh which substitutes for something ruder while drawing attention to the self-restraint on the part of the person doing the sigh.

'Let's get to something useful,' she said.

'I'll decide what's useful,' I said.

She found this so surprisingly arrogant that it almost made her laugh.

'I'm deadly serious,' I said. 'This is what I do for a living. I'm trained and practised at it. You know shag all about it and have never been trained for it, so you won't dictate what happens, OK? Now either answer the question or go, right now.'

'I was thinking that it's probably a version of that old thing, "Everybody's out of step but our Johnny." That if everybody else thinks I'm negative and pessimistic and depressed, then maybe I am.'

'Everybody doesn't think you're depressed. Depressing, yes. Depressed, no. And while you're dealing with me, show me the basic courtesy of sitting up straight and looking at me.'

She slithered into a more upright position and asked if she was permitted to ask me a question. I nodded.

'What did *you* think about me between the last meeting and this one?'

'Not that much, to be brutally honest, because I deal with perhaps six people in any one week in coaching contexts. I tried to figure how I could best help you, which led me to wonder if you wanted to be helped, if you wanted to change, or if you were unhappily happy with your current reality. I don't mean the prospect of losing another job. I mean the prospect of just continuing the way you're going. And I was trying to figure if you've chosen to be deliberately negative about everything – and if so why – or if you're negative without intent, like someone with Aspergers who isn't being unfeeling when they don't look a friend in the eye, it's just they're wired wrongly. And then wondering which of those two you'd prefer it to be – you choosing to be a negative force in your own and countless other lives, or you being a negative force without having any control over it whatsoever.'

At that precise moment, two things happened. She began to laugh and HaiYing walked in with a tray. HaiYing's expression changed not a whit, although she must have been surprised, since in all the preceding weeks, during which HaiYing would have brought her to one of our meeting rooms, Suzanne had never smiled. Not once. So whole-hearted laughter was a surprise. When HaiYing had left, Suzanne said that she did not set out to be negative and was for the most part unaware that she was being so. She also, she added, had deep reservations about false smiles and don't-worry-be-happy self-help crap.

'I know,' I said sympathetically. 'All positive-thinking bullshit dreamed up by capitalism to convince exploiters that the exploited are happy out. The way slave owners loved to have their saves singing in the cotton fields.'

She started to nod, then subverted it by putting her head on one side and glaring at me.

'I'm not that simplistic.'

'And I'm not selling you anything. I don't care if you continue the way you are. You're not a friend of mine. You're a client. And while I'd be sorry to know that you went out of here determined to continue to reduce the sum of human happiness…'

'That's an outrageous thing to say. I don't reduce the sum of human happiness.'

'Yeah, you do. Every day. Starting with yourself. You're not happy and you've never mentioned to me even a fleeting moment of happiness. But then you move on to other people – in your past and present jobs, people decided you were a "dead-catter". Everybody's heart sinks at the approach of a dead-catter. Everybody starts looking for ways to get out of the room and away from them. That's reducing the sum of human happiness, one company at a time.'

'How shallow and glib.'

'Tell me something. Does it make you feel better to call me shallow and glib?'

'It's the truth.'

'Maybe so. Although Da Vinci did say that simplicity was the ultimate sophistication. Does saying I'm shallow and glib make you feel better and if so, why?'

She was silent, her mouth, downward-turned at the corners, answering the question for her. I talked to her about the false promises of the self-help books that claim to be able to remove loneliness, fear, stammers or insomnia if the reader subjects themselves to a set regimen, then moved on to the development of positive psychology, pointing out that most students of mental health have tended to look at the unwell and the unhappy as a way of understanding the human condition and that it is only in the last twenty years that pioneering individuals like Martin Seligman and Harvard scholar Tal Ben-Shahar have flipped the coin and concentrated instead on happy and successful people in order to find out what they do that can be emulated by those of us who may not – from birth – be naturally happy.

'Three tasks before the next meeting,' I said. 'And don't argue or start looking for evidenced justifications. If you do them, we can look at the rationale next week. If you don't, it's not going to matter anyway. First thing, find a way to say something positive in the course of a meeting. Any meeting. Each and every meeting. Make a note of what you say, of the context and what happened as a result. Second thing, write a letter to someone who was good to you, thanking them. Thirdly, make contact with someone you know you should be closer to and meet them.'

The following week, you expect me to tell you, Suzanne arrived with a spring in her step, her face wreathed in smiles, whistling a tune as she climbed the stairs. Sorry. Ms Greene was unchanged.

'This stuff just took up so much time,' she said, as I started to make notes. 'I'm sure you think it's all very simple: just do X and Y and Z and then you move on to someone else and *I'm* not your problem any more because I'm all set up on these little self-improvement tasks. But I take this seriously and I gave it due consideration and – for example – writing a letter to someone is not what I would do, I mean it's just not *me*. Also this off-the-top-of-your-head suggestion that I would –

I flagged her into silence while I wrote the end of the last sentence she'd said.

'Make notes,' I said. 'Don't argue. Don't ask questions, just make notes. Point one: stop denigrating what other people say to you by characterising it from the outset as "stuff" or calling it "these little tasks" or describing it as "off-the-top-of-the-head suggestions".'

I waited for her to finish writing and asked her to read it back, correcting what she'd missed or skewed.

'Secondly, don't waste your time dismissing this as personal sensitivity from me. I don't give a sugar, one way or the other. But I know bloody well that the sheer fluency, the very ease of your verbal abuse means that it's a habit applied all day, every day to other people, some of whom *do* care and *are* vulnerable to it. Thirdly, stop complaining. Just stop complaining. You complain all the time. Most of the shit in life is a given and shouldn't be made more important than it is by whingeing about it. Fourthly, stop insulting other people by implying that what they do is easy/lazy/shallow/spurious or in some inchoate way less valid than what you do. Finally, stop defining who you are by the worst of yourself. You're not the kind of person who ever writes a letter of gratitude? What does that say about you? How clever is it to decide that a lousy self-absorbed track record is the template for the future? Now you're out of here. Come back when you've done the tasks as laid out, or come back to Steph saying we're done. I'll leave you to finish off your notes.'

One week later, she was back, three tasks completed.

'First of all, the meeting,' she began. 'I tried to do more than you had stipulated, by watching people, and whenever I thought they were even half-reasonable in the points they were making, nodding or trying to look extra interested. Then when one of the guys, Oliver, suggested a particular course of action, I waited until a couple of other people had nearly killed the idea with grudging acceptance and then I came in and specified a way it could be made to happen and why it would be worth doing. Minuted.

Second thing was the letter of gratitude. I sent a letter to a man in my previous company who had done his best when the tide turned against me. I told him that I never saw it coming, that I knew he *had* seen it coming and that, therefore, trying to defend and promote someone who could miss something so obvious was extra kind of him. I apologised for never being in touch with him in the intervening years and said I only recently understood the difficulties I had caused him. I got a reply by courier. I had posted mine. He sent me a reply within an hour – well, I imagine it was that quick – after he got mine and it was a lovely letter wishing me well and saying – well, wishing me well. He actually said that he always knew that once I got out of my own way nothing would stop me.'

She sat silent for a while thinking about the letter and I shut up, because the atmosphere was as fragile yet heavy as it gets before an electrical storm.

'He – it was – the way his letter was written, it was as if he thought me writing to him meant I had got out of my own way. He was that sure. That – that hopeful. Oh fuck.'

She was crying and fighting it. This was not the time to touch her or sympathise. I shoved tissues at her and waited.

'Third thing,' she said, way too soon, her voice still shaking, 'was r-r-reaching out to someone. I went to see my sister.'

She said nothing more. Just did a 'go on' gesture. If she didn't see the encounter with her sister as something to be explored, that was fine with me.

'Assume where you got to at the meeting was a two out of ten,' I said. 'See if you can get to a six next week and make notes of where it works and doesn't work.'

Before I could add anything to that, she was up and headed for the door. The following week, she explained that she had embarked on writing letters to everybody she had ever found inspirational or who had taught her anything. And she was making contact with lost friends. She would not need to take up my time so much, she said, but she'd talked to Damien and he said his PA would make an arrangement with The Communications Clinic – if I was willing – which would mean she would report to me weekly in a one-page email and drop in to see me occasionally. I was relieved that Damien seemed to view Suzanne as being with him for the long haul.

'Report to me every week?'

'That sounds like I'm inviting you to police me. I'm not. I don't care if you don't even read what I send to you. Just – having to send it to you regularly – it'll keep me disciplined.'

That's what she did. Over the next year, she did markedly better at work, as evidenced by two six-monthly appraisals, which noted her being more flexible and more willing to adapt to changed circumstances. She sniffed at this finding, believing that 'willingness to adapt to changed circumstances' is management-speak for 'does what she's told and doesn't whinge about it' and that when she was perceived as whinge-of-the-year she was in fact doing the company a service by drawing management attention to implications of their change agenda to which they might not have paid enough attention. However, if they didn't want to be warned and were likely to cast such warnings as unfortunate behaviours specific to her, then she would give them what they wanted: positivity.

It would be much more satisfactory to report that Suzanne,

over the year after she first came for coaching, radically changed her attitude and beliefs, thereby enhancing her career and personal wellbeing. Happily ever after is the ending we want to all narratives and this expectation has been reinforced down the year by self-help books, starting with Norman Vincent Peale's *The Power of Positive Thinking*. Anne Frank said that we all live with the objective of being happy and Suzanne Greene's story would tick more boxes if she underwent a profound and fundamental change, turning her into a glowing, charismatic Pollyanna.

That wasn't what happened. Suzanne is still a stranger to happiness and optimism but she knows that positivity is an essential lubricant in her workplace and that her pervasive negativity does nobody – especially not herself – any good. She is therefore committed to mechanically delivering on a list of daily targets. She now accepts that more people get persuaded into virtue than reproved out of vice but choosing to walk on the sunny side of the street will never come naturally to her.

'You'd probably prefer me to do a Road to Damascus conversion but that's not going to happen,' she said at one stage. 'Anyway, I've never understood why Christians get so worked up about the story of Saul getting blasted off his horse and falling on his head and deciding he was a bad guy for persecuting Christians. Sure, he was converted, but a lot of people would be converted by a heavy blow to the head. He just did the same stuff under a different banner. I'm not a convert. It doesn't make sense to me that people won't listen to you unless you lick them like a collie. I am enjoying work much more than I was eighteen months ago but that's because I've surrendered. Not been converted. Surrendered. If that's the way I have to act in order to be heard, get good appraisals, get a bonus, then that's how I'll act.

'But it's like I've learned a second language – it's not what first occurs to me and I have to concentrate harder. I'm never going to be a native speaker of positivity and there's no particular satisfaction in getting the reactions I get – the more open, the warmer reactions. If you want the truth, there's always going to be a part of me that has nothing but contempt for how easily bought they are. Bought. Cheap. Praise them or say they've made a good point instead of, "If you thought that through, you'd realise it's barking," and they're yours. What gives me satisfaction is learning a new skill. Like changing the tyre on my car. It happens to be a complicated process with a special key and I don't have to do it often but I like knowing that I can, that I have done it enough times to be able to rely on my capacity to do it again immediately, if I have to. Same thing with positivity. I make notes at every meeting and once I have a score of five, I can relax a bit. I make a list each morning of people I have to be nice to and I do it and I know people would say how mechanistic but most of the stuff – most of the good stuff we do every day is mechanistic. Businesses make profits because their employees get up at the same time and come to work by a set time, not because staff leap out of bed all excited by the impulse to go to work. If I tell one of my reports that she did a really thorough job producing a document and that it's a marked improvement on anything the department previously produced, what does she care that she was Number 2 on my Tuesday list? Even if she knew? That's actually where the satisfaction is for me. Doing something that has measurable results and doing it in a measurable way. When I report to you, I don't want or need praise. Or get it. You're just the scorecard that keeps me doing it.'

In print, some of what Suzanne says about the way she operates sounds grim, grey and – as she herself puts it – mechanistic. But, as a trainer, I'm sceptical about total smack-upside-the-head conversion. Every one of our trainers in The Communications Clinic has delivered a course that has changed people and sometimes companies will come back to us saying that their internal 'smile sheets' – the questionnaires staff fill in after courses – generally showed a high satisfaction level but that one of the participants said that we had changed his or her life and that they would be quite different from now on.

We love to hear it but we never claim it as an outcome of any course, past or future, and never have. Because, although people may experience a joyous breakthrough on a course, although they may see themselves quite differently as a result of their involvement, it's wise to remember the weight-loss analogy. That's where an obese individual gets jolted, whether by the sight of an unflattering photograph, a catcall in the street or a health warning from a GP, into losing weight. They muster their willpower and go through all the phases of weight loss, down to the triumphant point where they can throw out the 'fat' clothes with the elasticated waists and accept the plaudits of friends, co-workers and acquaintances, albeit with that little voice of doubt at the back of their amygdala, that wonders, in a bothersome whisper, if everybody hated the weight loss hero when they were fat? The problem with this story of conversion, resolution, dedication and achievement is the postscript. The majority of weight-loss heroes gain it all back and then some. Conversion and conviction aren't enough.

Nothing matches the dogged power of habit. Replacing a bad habit with a good habit does more for health and happiness than all the motivational speeches in the world. Suzanne Greene has largely replaced a bad habit with a good habit. Because she's now been doing it each day for more than three years, noting down when she registers herself doing it and sending me the total at the weekend (yes, she still does that), she has, whether she knows it or not, built up, not a reflex of positivity, but a reflex causing her to reject her instinctive negativity. I doubt if she'll ever instinctively be positive but does that matter to the co-workers who no longer duck into toilets when they see her headed for their offices, out of dread at her 'dead-catting'?

The motivation behind a good deed isn't as important as

the doing of the good deed. Imagine you're involved in a road accident and are bleeding out from a deep arterial cut when someone trained in first aid pulls away the crushed car door, yanks off their belt and gets an effective tourniquet around your damaged limb. The motivation on the part of the rescuer may be nothing more than the desire to deliver on the St. John's Ambulance course they did years back, or to show off to the other, less competent bystanders. As long as this bloke is keeping your blood inside you where it belongs, you're just grateful.

Suzanne did her own version of the tourniquet. When I walked into a blizzard of bad publicity at one stage, a table-top arrangement of flowers arrived one day with a short but insightful and thoughtful letter to the effect that this, too, would pass and that a year later I would find it difficult to remember just how painful it had been. It didn't matter to the recipient of the letter – in this case me – that writing it might be part of a coaching exercise and that the sender – Suzanne – might tick it off a list at the end of the day. And Suzanne's list-making may, ultimately, be more rewarding to her than the unjustified internal narrative some people have, which features them – à la St Paul – rising to great challenge.

Or, as T.S. Eliot puts it in *Four Quartets:*

Footfalls echo in the memory
Down the passage which we did not take
Towards the door we never opened
Into the rose garden. My words echo
Thus, in your mind.
But to what purpose
Disturbing the dust on a bowl of rose-leaves
I do not know.

CAREER PITFALL #7: NEGATIVE THINKING

Most negative thinkers have no clue how destructive their frequently articulated pessimism is to the humour of those around them and to their own career progress. Some negative thinkers are like Mrs Gummidge, believing their negativity makes them deeper, wiser and more sensitive than others. Mrs Gummidge, you will recall, was the 'lone, lorn creetur' in Dickens's *David Copperfield*, who burst into tears when the fire smoked and, when it was pointed out to her that everybody in the room was equally inconvenienced, said that she felt it more. 'Wot's the good of anyfink? Nuffink,' was the theme of her life.

Some negative thinkers have the wit to shut up about their bleak prognostications and some are not permanent pessimists but occasionally hit a downswing. Look at it this way. If you're accosted by a researcher before you walk home tomorrow after work in the gathering dusk of the wonderfully longer evening and asked how you feel about the journey, the chances are that you'll take a positive view of it. If, on the other hand, you get mugged just as you arrive at your gate and are questioned immediately after you have been pounded and pillaged, your attitude will be somewhat more nuanced, not to say negative.

It's widely assumed that pessimism equals unhappiness. It does not. There's a great happiness in knowing you're right and studies repeatedly demonstrate that pessimists have much greater accuracy of prediction than optimists. They predict the worst. It happens – and they get to say, 'I told you so.'

Their lives are built on constant reinforcement of their good judgement, whereas the sweetness-and-light brigade spend half their time wiping egg off their faces. All that guff about picking yourself up, dusting yourself off and starting all over again ignores the reality that if you hadn't been such an irrationally optimistic twit in the first place, you wouldn't have to do all the self-dusting and personal reassurance.

Committed pessimists seek out the evidence to confirm their conviction that the worst will happen. Accordingly, as a fearful frequent flier and card-carrying catastrophist, I have amassed, down the years, an unequalled library of books about air crashes, whether caused by pilot error, mechanical failure or the self-sacrificial instincts of flocks of birds. I know by heart the black-box recordings of pilots struggling with problems in advance of ploughing into the nearest hill, each of them ending with, 'Oh, shit,' followed by the silence of extinction. When I was on a transatlantic airliner that developed the small problem of fire in the cockpit, I was able to run through all the permutations and dire possibilities in my head. Other passengers screamed and wept. I did calculations. More to the point, when the smoke-filled plane eventually landed at Shannon, I was quite disappointed when they put us on coaches for Dublin. I was positively eager to fly, figuring I would be totally protected by the law of averages. That's the great thing about pessimism. When the worst happens, it not only satisfies the lust for disaster but – like banging your head off a stone wall – makes for a most enjoyable aftermath.

Pessimists, as contributors to society, are gravely underrated. If we'd had pessimists in charge of our banks, we wouldn't be in the mess we're in. In fact, prospective board members of any bank should be tested for pessimism in advance of appointment in a process which would weed out the cheery hopeful contenders. This would not only protect shareholder value and prevent collusion with the kind of daft optimists who happily took on 100 per cent mortgages, but would make board meetings much more interesting.

Interesting? Pessimists? In the proper mix, yes. Or the proper context. Pessimists do well in fiction, where writers often make them much more interesting than optimists. Eeyore, the depressed donkey in *Winnie the Pooh*, with his droopy ears and general aspect of grey grimness, is much more appealing than the chirrupy characters favoured by modern writers for children.

Similarly, most readers of *The Hitchhiker's Guide to the Galaxy* secretly identify most with Marvin the Paranoid Android who expects, and invariably gets, tediously menial tasks to do. 'Brain the size of a planet and they ask me to do this,' he mourns.

What coaches and management consultants increasingly find – particularly since the economic meltdown – is that pessimism comes into florid relief when the natural pessimist stops feeling in control of their life and career.

This can happen for any one of a number of reasons, including an employer under financial pressure who starts to query every aspect of every employee's work.

If you're in a job where you have control over your own destiny, you may have to deal with fear and worry but you are not likely to suffer generalised depression or pessimism. You convert fear into activity. (Unless you're the moronic pilot who was sent to prison a couple of years back for enthusiastically engaging in loud prayer in the face of engine failure, so that instead of making for the nearest airport, he ended up killing many of his passengers in an unmanaged crash landing.)

Studies have shown that the queuing system in Disneyland, where they tell you in advance that you're stuck there for as long as forty minutes, does not lead to irritation or negative thinking. Customers have at least the illusion of control. They can choose to abandon that particular attraction and go to another with a shorter line leading to it.

The bottom line is control. Which means that an employer who's getting sick of a corporate dead-catter, instead of working up to a frenzied condemnation, should consider not addressing the negative thinking directly but structuring the employee's day so that they gain what Charles Duhigg calls 'a sense of agency':

'Simply giving employees a sense of agency – a feeling that they are in control, that they have genuine decision-making authority

– can radically increase how much energy and focus they bring to their jobs,' he maintains. 'One 2010 study at a manufacturing plant in Ohio, for instance, scrutinised assembly-line workers who were empowered to make small decisions about their schedules and work environment. They designed their own uniforms and had authority over shifts. Nothing else changed. All the manufacturing processes and pay scales stayed the same. Within two months, productivity at the plant increased by 20 per cent. Workers were taking shorter breaks. They were making fewer mistakes.'

The more control people have over their own lives, the less likely they are to bitch and moan about other people or about processes. In addition, it's worth pointing out that negative thinkers should be involved in teams and listened to. No matter how positive a company's culture is, its positivity should not be based on an unspoken determination to exterminate or at least extrude pessimists.

The pessimist is often the person who keeps companies on the right side of the law and workmates on the right side of an A&E trolley or a sexual harassment complaint. They know the rules. They're often well paid not just to know the rules but to make sure everybody else knows the rules too and abides by them.

What nobody can bear is the person who squelches possibility, who hates those with what Barack Obama called 'the audacity of hope'. If you are that kind of person, you can change.

You may have been born that way – there is some evidence to suggest that a downbeat pessimism running through a personality can be spotted in newborns – but that doesn't mean you can't develop the habits of an optimistic person. The man who pioneered positive psychology, Martin Seligman, says, 'A pessimistic attitude may seem so deeply rooted as to be permanent. I have found, however, that pessimists can in fact learn to be optimists.'

There's your cue. Get on with it.

Five Tips for You as Your Own Coach

1. Ask someone close to you to be your negative language monitor. Don't feel self-conscious about making this request. Everybody loves the chance to ride shotgun on someone else's bad habits and by alerting them to pessimistic language and its bad effects on relationships and communication, you are doing them a favour they can apply to aspects of their own life, now or in the future. Keep their focus narrow. Get them, for example, to alert you every time you start a sentence with 'But…' Concentrate on this until it simply never happens and you'll thereby have made your discourse more positive.

2. Never do the egregious 'reinforcement sandwich'. This is negativity dressed up as positivity. You praise someone to the skies, then slip a criticism shiv between their ribs, then praise them to the skies again. All that approach does is ensure that whenever you praise anyone for anything, they're waiting for the 'On the other hand' to hit them amidships.

3. At any business meeting, make sure your ratio of positives to negatives is five to one. And add chronology to the challenge. In other words, do not allow a negative to pass your lips until you have uttered five encouraging or reinforcing comments. You may panic that you can't think up enough positives to allow you to get to your cherished negative. What does this tell you, you little ray of sunshine, you?

4. Don't get into the habit of negative phraseology. One of the most frequently used and utterly pointless negatives emitted by radio presenters is, 'But first.' 'In today's programme,' the presenter will say, 'We'll be examining the illegal jelly baby trade, looking into how hedgehogs have sex and explaining how cursive handwriting started. But first…' Why the 'But'? Where's the dark contrast?

5. When preparing for any negotiation, whether in work or at home, concentrate on conditionality, because this is

where negotiations often founder. Because you have a good understanding of the context within which you're being asked to do something, you may tend to start with that.

'I can't go down in the woods today,' you'll say, 'without encountering louche teddy bears, because this is their picnic season and it screws with everything. I cannot possibly survey that area as you want me to with them everywhere.'

That statement brings everything to a halt. Put it positively, however and see how much easier forward progress becomes:

'D'you know what would make this work really well? If you could get the annual teddy bears' picnic shifted to Stephen's Green, in their absence, we could be in and out of those woods, task complete, in thirty-six hours.'

8

The Quiet One in the Corner

The voice was quiet but clear. The brief was brief but clear.

'My name is Aileen McNeill. I am likely to be promoted in the next six weeks and the woman who runs my section recommended I advance my people skills.'

'Which ones?'

'I don't shine in presentations and I say little at meetings.'

'Why?'

'I am reserved.'

'Why?'

'I have always been shy.'

'Good.'

For the first time, her eyes came up and she asked a question without asking a question. I indicated that having the insight and comfort to calmly claim shyness was rare and meant we were starting from a good shared reality.

Over the following weeks, Aileen, for the first time in her life, got to explore shyness and introversion as human traits, rather than as personal flaws. I gave her a copy of my own book, *The Fear Factor,* which includes a whole chapter on shyness. She read it and then read some of the original studies it was based on but, when she came for her second session, was still locked into the notion of herself as in some way failing to measure up to the norm. I asked her to work out the origins of this feeling and pushed her to find the first memories of it. She looked into space for a long, long time before eventually deciding that she had no specific memories.

'It's all the same,' she said. 'Around first Holy Communion, around school concerts, around the visit of the P.P. I don't remember being excluded or commented on, really. I was always herded into the safest place. Whoever was in charge assumed I shouldn't be put centre-stage, or first in line.'

It was possible, she felt, that she had been put in first place in the past but may have cried, hidden or gone speechless, so that teachers and others decided, 'That one's shy, hide her in the middle so nobody notices.'

'I was happy enough,' she told me. 'I never wanted to be noticed.'

As time went on, not wanting to be noticed became a daily imperative. That's how it happens with most shy people. Shyness seems to begin in the cradle.

In the 1960s, a psychologist named Jerome Kagan, studying children, realised that, while many babies go through a phase where the sudden arrival of a new face upsets them (so they 'make strange'), most get over it within months. However, in some children, shyness went much further than 'making strange'. He began to suspect that the only trait that stayed unchanged from the infant years to adulthood was a shy temperament. As time went on, Kagan became more curious about this 'behaviour inhibition' and picked out two contrasting groups of toddlers. One was made up of sociable, extroverted, talkative two-year-olds. The other was made up of inhibited, shy children of the same age.

Five years later, the children were tested again, the overwhelming majority of them were still inhibited: quiet, serious and more cautious than those in the control group. The same happened when they were tested five years later. Virtually no child who started out on their life path with a strong tendency towards shyness ever became a bouncy uninhibited teenager.

Jerome Kagan theorised that perhaps the amygdala of the shy children was more easily activated than that in more socially-comfortable children, so they were always on the verge of flight. Which raised the possibility that the shyness had been present since birth. After all, if it was consistent from the age of two until the mid-teens, it seemed a reasonable assumption that it had been present in the first years of life. So Kagan went even further back and found that two out of ten children, tested at four months, showed significant distress when subjected to a sudden noise or any unexpected stimulus. They weren't intrigued or entertained by the stimulus. They were inhibited and upset.

Three years later, the 20 per cent of children who had over-reacted to external stimulus turned out to be – yes, you've guessed it – shy. Kagan even went into the womb and was able to indicate that children with a raised heartbeat while still in there were likely to become easily over-stimulated babies and, in turn, shy toddlers.

Finally, he looked at the families of children who were shy and found that the parents of shy toddlers tended themselves to be socially inhibited. So social phobia or shyness runs in families. It doesn't always follow, any more than red hair follows from one generation to the next, but it's an increased likelihood, just as, in the case of identical twins, if one of the pair is a social phobic, there's a one in four chance the other will be, too.

Social phobia appears in most cultures and is widely distributed, but knowing others are in the same pickle doesn't help you if the very thought of dating makes you blush and the thought of eating in front of someone else turns you scarlet.

Coming back a week after reading the book, Aileen was carrying a hardback called *Quiet* bu Susan Cain, on a related topic, which should be read by all reserved or shy or introverted people. Aileen had put two of those sticky flags at the beginning and end of her favourite passage from the book:

'We live with a value system that I call the Extrovert Ideal – the omnipresent belief that the ideal self is gregarious, alpha and comfortable in the spotlight. The archetypal extrovert prefers action to contemplation, risk-taking to heed-taking, certainty to doubt. He favours quick decisions, even at the risk of being wrong. She works well in teams and socializes in groups. We like to think that we value individuality but all too often we admire one *type* of individual – the kind who's comfortable 'putting himself out there'. Sure, we allow technologically gifted loners who launch companies in garages to have any personality they please but they are the exceptions, not the rule, and our tolerance extends mainly to those who get fabulously wealthy or hold the promise of doing so.

'Introversion – along with its cousins sensitivity, seriousness and shyness – is now a second-class personality trait, somewhere between a disappointment and a pathology. Introverts living under the Extrovert Ideal are like women in a man's world, discounted because of a trait that goes to the core of who they are. Extroversion is an enormously appealing personality style but we've turned it into an oppressive standard to which most of us feel we must conform.

'The Extrovert Ideal has been documented in many studies, though this research has never been grouped under a single name. Talkative people, for example, are rated as smarter, better-looking, more interesting and desirable as friends. Velocity of speech counts as well as volume: we rank fast talkers as more competent and likable than slow ones. The same dynamics apply in groups, where research shows that the voluble are considered smarter than the reticent – even though there's zero correlation between the gift of gab and good ideas.'

By the end of our sixth session, Aileen was quietly comfortable about taking on the communications exigencies of her new job because of the confirmation of something she had always believed: that extroverts are often over-rated and introverts under-rated in business. Now it was time to tackle her presentation skills. She brought a recently delivered presentation, PowerPoint slides and all. As she delivered it, it was bad. Seriously but dully bad. It felt as if it would never end. Both of us needed coffee when it was over. She opened a Kit-Kat and took quiet pleasure in running an elegant nail down the middle of the silver foil. I asked her how she'd gone about building the presentation.

'It's a corporate presentation,' was the answer.

'I don't follow?'

'The PowerPoint was passed on to me and I had seen someone else do it a few times.'

This presentation-by-hand-me-down should never happen but goes on in all sorts of companies and in state-sponsored bodies, such as the one this woman worked in. If you think about it, it's a practice that disrespects each audience by assuming they're all the same. Aileen seemed surprised but not worried by my outrage at the idea of her organisation having a one-size-fits-all presentation, pointing out that other executives within the organisation possess-ed of more personality than her tended to make it work all right, although she often wondered how effective it was for the purpose for which it was designed. She finished off the Kit-Kat, opened up her folder and sat, pen poised.

'The essential thing to do when you have to make a major presentation is just about the last thing most presenters do: start at the end,' I said.

'Start at the end?'

'Yes. Work out the outcome you want (over and above simple survival and I'll get to that later). Do you want your team or your boss to do something as a result of your presentation? Do you want your listeners to understand something differently?'

She began to make notes. Detailed, unhurried notes. She was going to capture for good anything she perceived to be worthwhile in what was said. When she finished that particular note, she nodded at it.

'It is obvious once it has been pointed out, isn't it?' she said, smiling. 'If you're not clear on what you want to come out of a presentation, how can you measure your own success or failure?'

'So?'

'So I should – everybody really should – write down the end result I would like to achieve before I start and then work out how to get to that point. It might be even better,' she ventured, 'if I talked to some of the audience first to find out what they wanted?'

'That a statement or a question?'

She considered this for a lengthy period of time.

'A statement.'

Laughing quietly, she made a note of that, too, before announcing with an air of challenge that a friend had told her she should make a joke at the beginning of any speech because it was the infallible way of getting audience attention.

'And your reaction to that advice?'

'I wouldn't be good at telling jokes.'

'Thanks be to God. Is your friend who gave you the advice?'

'Is he what?'

'Good at telling jokes?'

'No.'

'I rest my case.'

'You haven't set out a case.'

That made me laugh, which in turn made her laugh. Not being obliged to start presentations with jokes seemed to be a great relief to her.

'Next time you do a presentation – sorry, let me backtrack. You're going to prepare a different presentation for the next time you visit us here, OK? First of all you're going to identify the real-life audience you'd expect for it. You're going to talk to some members of that audience to find out what they need to know, what they need to understand, what they need to do as a result of your presentation, right? Then you're going to work out what they need to hear that will achieve these objectives. The first contrast with today that we should see next time we record you is not you coming on like a stand-up comic but something much simpler. This recording shows you greeting them with your head down as you read out those words that are *so* difficult to remember: 'Ladies and Gentlemen.' Next time, you'll greet them warmly and get their attention by looking as if you're in charge and by cutting to the chase. Tell them the single most interesting thing first. People are interested in what affects them, so find a point within what you've decided they must understand and put it at the top. After that, concentrate on being interesting, understandable and memorable.'

We then went through the DVD, which was made easier by the earlier discovery that Aileen had been delivering a presentation she didn't originate, since most of the problems that surfaced were inherent in the handed-on semi-script. Here's an example that made me push the stop button on the playback machine:

'The subject of implementation has been addressed by the team because it was felt that the significant change required within the organisation could not be effected exclusively at the strategic level but almost by definition, should be implementable.'

Even in print, you have to admit, that's not easy to understand. Coming at an audience in real time, it would be even less so. That's because it's in conceptual language. Conceptual language doesn't work in the spoken word. When we encounter it in the written word, we can stop, look up at the ceiling and work out what we *think* it means. But we don't have this luxury when listening to the spoken word.

This was another oddity of that inherited presentation – it was completely in the written word, rather than the spoken word, making whoever faithfully presented it sound like a robot. (Those who rose above it, according to Aileen, tended to be less than faithful to the script, which suggested that they were wise as well as having more in-your-face personalities than she had.)

The spoken word is a distinct language. It uses short sentences.

Simple words. Lots of illustrations and examples. And not saying anything in a presentation you wouldn't say to another individual. People don't become more amenable to boredom/being patronised/confused just because they're in a group.

The best way to make points understandable and memorable is to illustrate them with details or put a story around them. If, for example, you're talking about managing customer complaints, try to find an example of where someone on your staff managed such a complaint superbly. A real, local and recent example always beats an example from a business book like the one about Nordstrom and the tyre. Nordstrom being an American department store that does customer service better than almost any other corporation. One of their war stories is of a man who arrived to their complaints department livid about the poor performance of a tyre. He was apologised to. They listened to his saga respectfully and said it must have put him in a dreadful position. Then they asked if it would be acceptable to offer him a refund, to which he huffily agreed. After he was gone, a trainee staffer pointed out to the complaints' manager that Nordstrom don't sell tyres. The manager nodded and made the point that if the customer *believed* he'd bought it there, all that would be achieved by proving him wrong was to humiliate him and make him angry at Nordstrom for quite a different reason.

It's a good story but if you tell it to an Irish audience, they smile cynically and decide that sort of scenario would be unrealistic in this country. When I told Aileen about Nordstrom, the evident contrast between her state-sponsored body and the American retailer seemed to delight her.

'We think we're among the top among state-sponsored bodies when it comes to customer service but we'd kind of fall short there. But I take the point.'

'Next time, by the way, as well as listening to the audience in advance, you'll listen to them throughout the presentation. The great thing about an audience is that they'll always tell you what they're thinking – *if you're looking at them*. Watch an audience and their expressions will help you judge how you're doing. They'll tell you, loud and clear, "Got that, move on." Or, "Sorry, don't quite follow." Or, "OMG, that's *so* true." Of course, you can't watch your audience if you use PowerPoint, which is why an awful lot of speakers use it.'

'In my organisation, if you made a presentation without PowerPoint – well, it never happens, but if you *did* make a presentation without PowerPoint, they would think you were just winging it. It would not be approved of.'

I shrugged. PowerPoint is a vile distracting disaster which should be used only when the audience needs to be talked through a chart or a technical process which requires them seeing the different elements within the concept. Maybe one out of every ten PowerPoint presentations happens for good reasons. Most of them happen for lousy reasons and anyone who can do their presentation without PowerPoint should do it that way.

'If you *must* use PowerPoint, don't start with it. Get the presentation structured so you know what follows what, beginning to end. Then – and only then – create PowerPoint slides. As few as possible,' I told Aileen. 'Rehearse by talking it out loud – that's a great way to reality-test a presentation. The bits you fall over or can't remember are the sections needing attention. Oh and I don't care how shy you are, don't do the looking out from under the eyelashes bit – the hanging head performance. No audience is your enemy. Every audience comes to a presentation or a conference speech with the simple hopes that a) they'll hear something useful, b) they won't be bored. Meet those two requirements and you'll be fine. Exceed them and enjoy the interaction and you'll be stellar.'

Aileen said this was all clear and encouraging but that she would be incredibly nervous the next time, trying to put into place all these new rules. In fact, a week later when she made the new presentation, she wasn't nervous at all. Or if she was, it didn't show. After she had seen the immeasurably improved performance on the DVD, she said she had found it easier to remember and think through a presentation she had created herself, that it more logically followed her own thought processes than did the inherited presentation. As we moved to address her performance at meetings, much the same change happened, not because she was praised or encouraged to contribute to meetings but because, once she analysed what she wanted to achieve at each meeting, it stopped being a process at which she was a cowed witness and became one she could influence and even – perish the thought – enjoy.

CAREER PITFALL #8: SHYNESS, INTROVERSION
This one's an pitfall because the twenty-first century is in love with extroversion. Don't accept this, if you're an introvert. Don't promote it, if you're a manager with an introverted employee.

Five Tips for You as Your Own Coach
1. Being an introvert doesn't permit you to be discourteous. Look people in the eye and give them a warm handshake.
2. Get good at presenting. Remember that you are trying to get ideas or information from your head into someone else's. This doesn't require you to perform as if you were in a pantomime.
3. Don't damp down your shyness with drugs or drink. Concentrate on the needs of others. It's not about you. It's about them.
4. When you're stuck with people in a social setting and think you might die from shyness, interview the people around you.
5. Use your introversion. Don't sit there silently feeling miserable because you haven't contributed to a meeting. Listen, pay attention and see if you can help those present get the most out of it.

9

The Rising Star Who Became Supermom

One of my favourite clients, for about ten years, has been a woman with a *basso profundo* voice, hair dyed the colour of Ribena and a uniquely personal way of starting a phone call. Doesn't matter if she rings on a landline or a mobile, it's the same. No greeting.

'Audrey. The thing is I find it interesting what the Swedes are doing with medical device costs,' she'll say.

None of that weak-kneed, 'Can you talk?' Or, 'Have I picked a bad time?' It may have been six months since the last conversation and this new one could be about what's going on in Syria, how the leadership in the CIA is changing the way it's making decisions, or how the carbon credit system for corporations is flawed. It's up to me to keep up. It's like stepping on to what you thought was a footpath only to find it's a moving walkway.

I worked with Audrey about ten years ago, when she decided she was going to make it to the top of her American-owned corporation but doubted that she had critical mass within the management of the day. She scoped out the issue like a five-star general and mowed down all opposition, which was why, when she rang me more recently, she was calling from Greenville, North Carolina, which is where the HQ of her company is situated.

'Audrey,' she said, as usual. And as usual moved straight on without permitting me to acknowledge presence, never mind state of health. I could be suffering from an advanced case of mange, hoose and worms, complicated by sudden-onset male-pattern baldness but as far as Audrey's concerned, when you answer your phone you're *ipso facto* confirming that you are fit for business.

'You'd'a met Sabina Hamilton that time in Toronto. Worked well.'

'Hang on. Is this the Amazon with the Marilyn Monroe voice?'

'That's her.'

'Shone like a lighthouse the whole three days and an absolute darling at the same time?'

'Her. Just married a Garda around that time.'

'Oh, I remember. You wanted to send her to Cambodia for four months?'

'Eight months. Before the Garda got himself shot in the arse.'

'What?'

'Do you not remember the thing that happened when a bunch of teenagers dug up an arms dump and one of the local Gardai did a Willie O'Dea for his friend's camera phone before putting the gun down with such force it went off and shot the friend in the arse?'

'He couldn't have expected the gun to be loaded or functional.'

'You *always* assume every gun is loaded and functional.'

'Audrey, what do you know about guns?'

'By the time I was fourteen, I could hit a dot on a ladybird at a hundred feet.'

'Right, so.'

'Minor flesh wound and then it goes septic and your man the husband's in intensive care and Sabina's out of the running for Cambodia. Fucksake. I sent Paul Collins. He did fine.'

I remembered Paul Collins. He is the sort of executive for whom the phrase 'a safe pair of hands' was invented. The kind of workmate who makes lists of pros and cons before coming to a measured decision, whereas Sabina would come to the same right decision in a flash of educated intuition. And then find a way to give the credit to someone else.

'So then Sabina gets pregnant.'

Audrey could not have used a more eyes-to-heaven tone of contempt if she'd been announcing that Sabina had taken to selling herself on the streets.

'This suggests that the Garda stopped being septic.'

'Like I give a…'

'No, you wouldn't, would you?'

'Sabina never even has an *hour's* morning sickness, tells the girls she wants no part of a shower, never gets into maternity clothes, just gets by with loose blouses, doesn't come in waving goddam scans and because your man's arse is healing slowly he's still off, so it'll be a short maternity leave.'

'Why do I think this is going to end badly?'

'Sprog popped. Septic Simon has a son. And next thing, seismic shift, Sabina's hit amidships by motherhood. Breastfeeding on demand, everything on demand, nothing matters but the sprog, don't ring or email and then two weeks before the end of the three months, hey presto a note saying she's taking the full entitlement and then whatever's left for free so she's gone for a year. When she comes back, we've Luis the Lunatic from Louisville in charge and she's way behind the eight ball but talk about hitting the ground running. Luis's about five foot four in platform shoes and hates tall people but makes the exception for Sabina so she's rising like a rocket and next thing she's up the spout for the second time.'

'Oh.'

'With, as it turns out, twins.'

'Well, twins could be a most efficient way to complete her family. Don't tell me. Another year gone?'

'Year and a half – six months compassionate leave because her mother was dying of Alzheimers and Septic Arse was unhappy.'

'About Sabina's mother?'

'*No*. He feels he's been passed over by the boys in blue so he takes some kind of disability package which at least means he can mind the children and let his wife get back to what she's good at but you know what? Golf. He may have a septic arse but he decides to develop a beeooriful swing, them being based up in Carlingford with a beeooriful golf course. Anyway, she's back seven months and I want her to head up Geneva and that's your job.'

This caught me completely off guard.

'Give me dates for coaching sessions, soon. Like yesterday.'

'I'll email you a few. I don't understand why Sabina'd need coaching. She's superb at everything she touches. I suspect her kids are the healthiest, most gorgeous around. What have you decided she needs in the way of a skills boost?'

'Her skills are grand. I want you to take her by the throat and tell her what I can't tell her without being sued. Tell her to make that fucker act like a father and get her act together and take Geneva and don't fuck around because that's what she's doing at the moment.'

'Does she want it?'

'Yes. Her fucking brain is fucking softened by motherhood, you know yourself. Scientific data proves pregnancy reduces a woman's brainpower by fifty per cent, temporarily.'

'The problem is that "temporarily" can mean six months or six years or sixteen years,' I said, recognising an old Audrey theme.

'Get her to understand this is the opportunity of a lifetime. No kidding, Tess, tell her I had to fight like a tiger to get to where I am and I'm offering her the same chance on a silver goddam salver. For your own information, I'm not telling anybody that I've offered it to her until I know she's good to go, because it's not gonna reflect well on me if I promote someone as fecund as fuck whose interest in the company is slim.'

During a small pause, I could hear Audrey summoning some-one into her office.

'That's not a problem,' she went on. 'I'll get someone good if I can't get her. But she'll never get anything as good again. Never get anything that'll stretch or reward her as much. She turns this one down, she's on the mummy track and nobody's fault but her own. And, of course, Septic Simon. Over to you. Bye.'

Within hours, Sabina had rung to set up an appointment. I described her to the people in my office who might encounter her.

'Six feet tall, long, *long* straight black hair like a mermaid. Breathtaking looks, tiny voice like a six-year-old, super competent and really likeable personality.'

The day she came, whoever brought her in arrived back in the front office looking puzzled.

'Thought you said she'd straight hair?'

'Not a bend in it.'

'Well, in that case she's had a perm. It's curly all over.'

'Nobody under sixty has perms.'

'Just saying.'

Sabina was unchanged since our previous encounter, other than the hair. Her pale face was surrounded by an explosion of black curls. It made her look completely different. She laughed when she saw my reaction.

'You can hate it or like it, not my fault either way,' she said. 'Pregnancy.'

'Huh?'

'First pregnancy, my hair went weird and wavy and started to fall out, so I cut it to shoulder length. Second pregnancy – curls.'

'Never heard of that happening, ever.'

'Me neither, but it did.'

I asked for the pictures and she ran them on her phone. She seemed to have the three happiest, most cod liver-oil-and-orange juice kids ever born. All girls.

'Their father says he's outnumbered.'

'He any good with them?'

'Oh, he adores them.'

That one was classic Sabina: a marvel of deflection from

the question asked. Casual listeners would assume hubby was wonderful at caring for the three toddlers but that wasn't what she'd actually said.

'Does he take care of them now you're back at work?'

'A lot, yes.'

'Every day?'

'My mum takes them on Tuesdays and Thursdays and Robbie's Dad on Wednesdays. Sometimes I get a student – she's the daughter of a neighbour – to help out. It's working really, really well. You'd be amazed.'

'Not with you in charge, I wouldn't.'

She didn't take up this invitation to contradict and say that her old man was in charge.

'How difficult was it to go back full-time?'

In fact, she admitted, it would have been impossible if she'd had to do it in one go but – thanks to Audrey's long-distance assistance – she had been able to come back gradually.

'So it's all "go",' she said. 'But honestly, this has been such a great time for us. They're dotes, so they are. Such *good* babies and they haven't really been sick at all or had accidents. Of course, they haven't been attending a crèche, so they didn't share germs. I breastfed them. Never thought I would but it worked out really well and I'm glad I did. I can't get over how different from each other they are and how quickly they're developing.'

Sabina was so joyfully enmeshed in her children's lives, it might have been expected that she would be less involved, less interested, when it came to discussing her work environment but, contrariwise, she was equally excira and delira about that. The company was expanding, it was involved in a new kind of partnership, the next ten years were going to be filled with thrilling possibilities and with luck Audrey would make it right to the top. With luck, because Audrey was a phenomenon. So clever, so motivational, so driven, so demanding. In the best sense, of course. Sabina counted herself as incredibly fortunate to have come, early in her career, under the aegis of so visionary a leader.

'Did you stay in contact with her when you were out of the office with the babies?'

'Do you know, I really intended to but everything seemed to happen in such a short time, I didn't. Not that I could have offered anything much because let's face it, I was out of the loop. And Audrey – well, the one thing you can say about Audrey and be sure she'd agree with, is that sentimental she isn't. So I don't think she'd have been crying into her coffee over me not ringing her!'

She poured me coffee and tea for her and wandered around the room.

'I loved your last premises but this is even nicer.'

'Sabina?'

'Hmmm?'

'D'you ever say anything negative about anything or any one?'

She sat down and considered this seriously. Wherever possible, she admitted, she tried to put things in a nice way, rather than giving out to people who made mistakes. As a manager, she found that encouraging people's strengths had a greater payoff than giving out to them about their weaknesses.

'I was really shocked – while I was out with the babies, I read a lot to try to keep up to speed, you know? And in one of the books I read about reengineering, this professor said that resistance to change was – I probably won't get the words exactly right but was something like 'the most annoying, puzzling, distressing and confusing'* aspect of corporate change. I was sorry for that professor. He seemed to be taking it so personally and seeing it like it was a flaw in everybody but him. Why would he see it as

---

* Former MIT Professor Michael Hammer, in *The Reengineering Revolution*, called the innate resistance to change of humans 'the most perplexing, annoying, distressing and confusing part of reengineering.'

a flaw? I mean, when someone gets Alzheimers, you try to keep the things that are familiar to them the way they are so they have security. I'm never happy when change management courses seem to criticise employees who are not willing to take a leap in the dark, even though I always come out well from the questionnaires.'

Sabina was talking about questionnaires administered as part of change management programmes, which claim to show up rigidity of personality inherent in some staff in any organisation. The theory is that this rigidity of personality militates against willing-ness on the part of those staff to embrace necessary change.

'The problem with those questionnaires is that people who answer questions about previous experiments with a firm reply to the effect that they really didn't work out and shouldn't have been tried in the first place *can be right*. Did you know that analysis of predictions from a prestigious think-tank in the States found 75 per cent of them were just plain wrong? My father had a book I remember because he was always saying it was published the year I was born — it was called *Megatrends* or maybe *Megatrends 2000* and it set out the ten big things that were going to shape everybody's future. Seven of the trends never transpired. Ever. To this day.'

That, she went on, was why a figure like Audrey was of such importance. Audrey didn't buy bullshit. Ever. She never went in for fads and she could spot a faddy person at ten kilometres. Audrey always said that most of the major directions in companies were logical extensions of what had happened in the past, not shocking changes, and that people were so transfixed by the arrival of the Internet that they got hazard-fixated.

'She got really cross, I heard, at a meeting recently, when one of her marketing people said we needed to be more on Twitter. She told him our products involved major strategic decisions taken over time by top management who didn't have the time to be reading random smartarsery on Twitter.'

'You hero-worship her.'

'Oh, yes.'

'So are you going to Geneva as she wants you to?'

She laughed and said she really, *really* wanted to and was working out how best to manage it.

'It's just a dream job,' she said. 'Great scope in it.'

'Explain the issue of managing it?'

'Well, I'll be going back to Audrey in the next few days with a proposal. I've checked flights and costs of accommodation and everything and by far the best option would be for me to fly out on Monday evening and come back on Thursday evening. Stay in an apartment close to the Geneva offices. And, of course, work in the Dublin office if necessary on Friday but generally I would think working from home would be the best way to consolidate the week. You know?'

I shook my head. No, I didn't know. Effectively, she'd be commuting and doing three days in Geneva?

'Well, I suppose if Audrey really felt it was necessary, I could fly out early on Monday. That would work.'

'Does this happen anywhere else within the corporation, that someone flies into the city…?'

Sabina shook her head and pointed out that up to relatively recently, the corporation had been very much dominated by men at the top and back in the day, the norm was for a man to up sticks and bring his family to live with him in his new location. But now that equality had broken out, thanks be to God, that no longer applied.

'Or has been reversed? Wives moving and their husbands and family going with them?'

That turned out to be a conversational lead balloon. Sabina politely walked around it and concentrated on the frequency of flights to Geneva. I pushed my iPad towards her. It was open at a page on which her company outlined its values, one of which was to be 'embedded and engaged in our communities'.

'Oh, yes, this is so important,' Sabina enthused. 'It's the only way to build up a relationship of trust between the company and those closest so they don't ever get fearful of the processes.'

I said nothing and she got started again about how her company was a leading influence on this. But with less impetus. Still smiling, still game, she ran out of words. Then, unexpectedly, she laughed.

'You don't think it's going to work, do you?'

'I can't help wondering why you wouldn't move to Geneva for a couple of years. Your children are way too young for school, your husband isn't currently tied down in a job...?'

'Ah, no. I can understand how it would look to someone like yourself but no, no.'

'Might look like that to Audrey, too? Why is it non-negotiable?'

'Just is.'

'So there,' I said, stamping my foot.

Sabina looked less happy and began to talk about 'the rights of others'.

'Robbie doesn't want to leave the golf course he's used to?'

For a moment, I thought she might take offence, but she chose to laugh.

'Oh, *you*. Robbie always wants to do the best for all of us. I just don't see it as fair that he should have to uproot himself from friends and family and the Ay – and other sup – everything.'

I closed my eyes to hear in my head what she had just said. The AA and other supportive networks? I didn't ask her but, considering the possibility that Robbie had an alcohol dependency problem, it might be suggested that getting him out of the location where he did his dangerous drinking would be a good, rather than a bad thing and that Geneva, in common with every European city, would have daily Alcoholics Anonymous meetings. So why was uprooting him so unthinkable? I got Sabina talking again but, other than an absolute conviction that removing Robbie from his home territory would not be a condign sentence, she revealed nothing else. I asked her if she thought Audrey would wear the commuting arrangement.

'Probably. She knows I'm the best for the job.'

'*Probably?*'

'You don't think so?'

'No – and neither do you, really. She's moved mountains for you already, allowing you to come back in a phased way. Anything more along those lines and it's going to look like favouritism. But quite apart from that, come on – if you were Audrey, would you be happy sending you off to Geneva knowing that over the next two years your children are going to get coughs, colds, earaches – all the usual joys of early childhood – and that they're going to want their mother first and foremost, *not, not, not* because she's female but she is the one who's always bandaged them and dosed them and taken them to the GP, right? And furthermore, when that happens, is Sabina Hamilton going to take a call from Robbie about Emma having the croup and say, 'Hey, take care of it, I'm here for the next two days,' or does she leap to her feet and catch the first flight home, urging the pilot to pick up the speed for Chrissakes?'

She laughed and nodded.

'If Emma *does* get croup, I'm going to blame you,' she added.

The two of us sat in companionable silence for several minutes.

'What am I being coached in, again?' she asked and laughed again.

'You pick.'

'Well, I think this has shown that I'm severely lacking in self-interrogatory skills. Took you bullying me to accept that Geneva's not going to be my job.'

'That *so* was not the objective.'

'Good, though.'

'How?'

She said that she realised she would be pushing her luck with Audrey, which would not be fair on Audrey but that even if Audrey consented to a commuter arrangement, she, Sabina, wasn't that sure she'd want it. 'Maybe when the loves are a bit older but not right now. Not right now.'

'I do need you to understand that Audrey would never have briefed me to push you towards this conclusion.'

'Audrey would want a number of things. She'd want me told to get the finger out, go to Geneva and begin the upwardly mobile path she travelled. She'd want you to identify the extra skills I'd need and help me develop them.'

She thought about what she'd said. 'But that's not going to happen. So I need to tell her quickly.'

I waited for her to think through what this would do to her corporate progress and therefore expected her to look sad. She didn't look sad. She looked ridiculously happy. Glowing, even.

'I'd've had to tell Audrey anyway,' she said, gathering her belongings about her. 'I'm pregnant again. So it's going to be career ticking over for a couple of years. Three, maybe.'

Audrey didn't come back to me with any comment about what Sabina told her, when Sabina told her. Audrey moves on to the next task. That's how Audrey's got as far as she's got. That – and not having children.

CAREER PITFALL #9: MOTHERHOOD

Babies undoubtedly create a career speed-bump. After one baby, continued upward career progress is possible. Two and your chances reduce. Three and it'll be a miracle if you make it to the top. But that's just commonsense.

Maternity leave takes a woman out of the workforce for several months. Repeated maternity leaves interrupt the way colleagues and superiors think about a woman. Especially if the new mother opts to extend her maternity leave or – if bitten by the marvellous motherhood bug – decides to take a year off. Or two years. The commercial caravan moves on. Nuthin' personal. The same would happen if it was a guy. Except – with one notable current transgender exception – men don't get pregnant.

The tendency of women to cooperate, rather than compete, is another factor. The TV programme *Why Men Don't Iron* took six little girls and a separate group of six little boys, giving each group an enviable toy. The little girls, in no time flat, evolved a method for sharing the toy equally. The little boys beat the living shit out of each other, with the winner taking complete ownership and awarded loans of the toy to the others, based on their behaviour and importance – to him.

It's a social reality that the behaviours that get young men into hot water – fights, public order offences, car crashes – are (if positively channelled) precisely the same behaviours that can lead to promotion in business: risk taking, competitiveness, ganging together.

Five Tips for You as Your Own Coach

1. Accept the statistics. Women find it easier to get to the top, globally, if they have no children or a small number of children.
2. Accept nature. Hurricanes and motherhood have a lot in common.
3. If you want to be an ongoing part of the team, stay in touch with the team while you're on maternity leave.
4. It (mostly) takes two to parent-tango. Develop joint policy around babies and how they'll be managed before they happen.
5. Don't prate about guilt. Do the best you can, babywise and careerwise and don't play that sympathy card. It never works.

10

The CEO Who Did the Right Thing

Marjorie wanted to get a job, after an interval outside the workforce and she wasn't ready, she told us when she contacted us, for specific job interview training. Maybe later. But first she needed someone – she didn't need training, really. But she wanted to talk out her options. With someone. Did that constitute coaching? If so, coaching was what she wanted.

When she arrived, she was in jeans and a top and carrying an oddly old-fashioned phone. One of those tiny flip phones that looked like the future just a few years ago.

'I'm told you know you don't want training or at least not yet but you want to talk stuff out,' I said, having introduced myself. 'So: talk.'

'I didn't think – sorry – I don't know where to start.'

'What was the last job you had?'

'I was running an event management company in Gloucester.'

'Were you good at it?'

'Yes.'

'Did you own the company?'

'No.'

'How long had you been there?'

'Four years, starting as an event manager, working up to CEO.'

'Managing how many?'

'Staffing in event management tends to be fluid. Could be twenty or forty, depending on what was going on.'

'Why Gloucester?'

'Personal reasons.'

'Meaning?'

'Partner. Boyfriend. Was from Gloucester.'

'Kind of family you come from?'

'Five siblings. Second youngest. My mother died five years ago.'

I looked at her and she looked at me. I couldn't figure what she wanted me to ask her or why she was so armoured against questions. So I told her the truth.

'I'm kind of lost. I have the feeling that you want me to ask you something specific that I'm missing. What is it?'

'Two years ago, my father had a stroke. January. He was living on his own. I came home the following day.'

'And?'

'Beaumont.'

That was not the answer that mattered, so I shut up and waited for the real answer.

'Never forget it. I'll never forget it. Never. My father's a words man. He was always a great talker. He was well-read and witty. He just was…and he was lying with his face kind of tilted to one side, like a candle melting.'

'Was he in distress?'

'No. That was the awful thing. He kept thinking things were funny, when they *so* weren't funny. I kept expecting him to be frustrated because he couldn't make sense when he was speaking to us. But he wasn't. He wasn't frustrated. He wasn't at all. He thought it was the craic.'

Hospital staff explained to her that a stroke can sometimes skew a sufferer's sense of what's serious and what isn't but predicted that her father's mood and attitude would probably change over the following weeks. She went back to her job, returning to Dublin for a bedside conference four days later.

'My brothers and sisters are there and it's six days after the stroke and the hospital can't wait to get rid of him. I'm not joking you. He's lying there, incontinent. His face is all collapsed to one side. He's speechless and he's laughing, although much less, and they want him out of there. They never use un-PC terms like 'bed blocker' but that's what they mean. And my big brother the priest is standing there nodding, nodding. I said to him, I said, 'Why should we want to take him out of the hospital? Isn't it their job to make him better?' And the social worker or bed manager or whoever the hell she was went on about how recovering from stroke was a long-haul job, took a long time and an acute bed wasn't appropriate. She used that word like a get-out-of-jail card. It and all applicable variations to it Appropriate. Inappropriate.'

What maddened her most was the behaviour of her older brother. Nearly twenty years older than Marjorie, Christopher was the family hero, the one brought in to mediate in disputes and talk reason to her when, as a teenager, she hit a rebellious period characterised by substance-abuse and cutting classes.

'And now he's standing there, all sweet reason, putting words in their mouths. Telling them they couldn't afford – that he "quite understood" that they couldn't afford to have beds taken up by old people. Old people. Category. Annoying category. He says this in front of my father as if – as if – because my dad can't talk he can't hear. But he could hear and he did hear his son the padre selling him right down the river and there wasn't much laughing out of him after that. Like you lose the right to be cared for or cured because you're in your seventies?'

Her father was put into a nursing home and when she visited at Christmas, she found her father uncomfortable but unable to explain why. She rang several times for a nurse, eventually going out on the main floor of the nursing home and flagging one down. That nurse told her that her dad probably wanted to go to the toilet but he'd be fine, he had an adult diaper on. Flummoxed, she asked the nurse if she was leaving this dignified old man to pee in his own bed and the nurse said she'd get to him but they were short-staffed that day because of flu.

'I just took him home. Right then and there. Wrapped him up and took him home. Rang the owner of my company in Gloucester and told him he'd have to give me six weeks to sort things out.'

She then called the family together and met with a collectively horrified response to what she had done. It was wrong, they told her, and their father would have to go back to the nursing home because none of them could take on the task of looking after him. They had commitments, they pointed out.

'That meant they were married, they had children – they'd been *unselfish* enough to have children. The great let-out, children. Never have to take responsibility for anything once you have the child in your arms. Can't put out your fire, have to mind my kids. Can't visit you when you're dying – my eldest has bronchitis. Can't take responsibility for my father, my youngest is making her First Communion. Kids are a licence for selfishness and I didn't have that licence and if I was going to take *rash, unconsidered unilateral action*, well…rearing families doesn't stop them having holidays and bridge nights and updating their Facebook pages and getting their kids tested for allergies but it does stop them taking on any wider responsibilities.'

The priest, apparently in a spirit of peacemaking, laid out the options. Their father could be returned to the same nursing home. Or Marjorie could identify a better nursing home and see if it had vacancies. Or she could take leave of absence from her job and take care of their father at home, supported, of course, by the rest of the family. When Marjorie told him the company for which she worked wasn't big enough or rich enough, in recessionary times, to offer even their most valued employee sustained compassionate leave, Geraldine, one of her sisters, remarked that she should have thought of that before she stepped in and decided to play heroine.

'My problem, Dad suddenly was. *My* problem. I have no

responsibilities, see, so it's up to me. I *was* living with a man and I had planned on spending the rest of my life with him but as far as the rest of them were concerned, if I wasn't in holy wedlock, it didn't count.'

Within six months Marjorie had lost her job in England, lost her lover and lost any sense of the future. She was nursing a disabled old man who had recovered only a little of his speech and who was deeply depressed.

'Being stuck in the house with a parody of what he was, it just ate a hole in me. And the others patronising me and saying I was marvellous. In the beginning, I had this curious illusion that it didn't matter, that it was just an interval, a rehearsal for something. I was so busy it took a while to sink in – this could go on for ten *years*. Month after month, I was losing more and more contacts, more and more confidence, eating junk, getting slobby and fat, letting the roots grow out because why would I do anything else? And I developed this awful hearty cheeriness because I couldn't have a conversation with him. So I could hear myself saying, "Let's get you up and about, then, Dad," and him looking hunted and me letting on to be happy, happy, happy. A rat in a cage with a halo.'

Her brother the priest would come to their parents' home, as she put it, 'religiously' once a month. The other siblings dropped in for an hour now and again.

'Big bloody deal that they let me up to Dublin for a day or so, now and again. Do you know what happened the last time I did that? More than a year and a half after I brought him home? My sister came over and I had a puncture on the M50, which is actually not the worst place to have a puncture. They send out trucks to help but it all takes time, so I was hours later than I had promised. You with me? At some point in the afternoon, early on, I think, my father needed cleaning up. She couldn't bring herself to clean him up. She was too sensitive. She was too sensitive and she knew he'd be very sensitive too. She's so sensitive, my beautiful sister, that she left her father sitting in his own shit for three hours. Reeking. Fucking *reeking*. When I got home I cleaned him up immediately. It wasn't soon enough. He wouldn't look at me. You know the phrase "Turning his face to the wall"? He did that. He literally did that. Not a look. He just retreated. He couldn't bring himself to be in contact with a world that would treat him like that. And his baby daughter? His baby daughter and a pillar of the community.'

A few silent months later, her father died in his sleep. Marjorie dealt with his funeral and – later – with the will. The house had been left to all of them and at a family gathering, her brother the priest suggested that Marjorie live there, rent-free, for a year, after which they could decide what to do with it. This appealed to the others because the property market had fallen on its nose and keeping Marjorie in the house until prices recovered a little meant that the house wouldn't deteriorate or attract squatters. That was six months ago.

'I've never told anybody any of this.'

'What about your former boyfriend?'

'What about him?'

'Did you not tell him any of it?'

'He didn't want to know. Anything. About it.'

'Did that surprise you?'

She looked at the floor in silence for some time before saying that her former boyfriend had probably welcomed the episode as a way of disengaging from her. He was now married to someone else, with whom Marjorie suspected he had already become involved before her father's stroke turned her life inside out. She didn't seem to care much.

I left the room and reappeared with coffee and slices of a chocolate nest cake my neighbour Mary Linders had made for me to bring into the office because it was the week after Easter. Marjorie began to laugh at the sight of the purple chick sitting spraddle-legged on her slice. She ate it with relish and downed a mug of coffee. I refilled her mug.

'So you never told anybody else about the last few years. You glad or sorry you told someone else now?'

'Glad.'

'Why?'

'Because I found out – you don't have to say anything. I mean, I'm not stopping you but I don't need you to be sympathetic or anything.'

'Oh, you think I'd be sympathetic?'

I deadpanned it and she began to laugh.

'I'm not sorry I did it.'

'Did what? Took your father home on impulse?'

That widened her eyes and she mouthed the word 'impulse'. Silently.

'Wasn't it?'

'What if it was?'

'For you to say.'

'"A snap decision but those are as good as any other, in my experience." Jack Reacher. I discovered Jack Reacher courtesy of my father. He had every one of the paperbacks. He nearly had another stroke the day I told him that Tom Cruise was playing Jack Reacher in the movie…Yeah. It was an impulse and it would've been a shitload easier on me if I hadn't done it.'

'Would it have been easier on your father?'

She sat back in silence. After a while, I looked at her and it was as if she was watching an unseen film – her eyes flicking from side to side.

'No. Honestly? No. Yeah, I could've reported the nursing home and done complaints but he would always have dreaded, dreaded, dreaded losing his freedom and being in a nursing home would've been the definition to him of losing his freedom. It might seem to an outsider that it didn't make much difference, him being at home in a bed. But it did make a difference. There were moments – there were moments, not of happiness, not of happiness in any real sense, but of laughter, of peace, of affection. Of remembering. No. Yes. It was right to bring him home and take care of him. Who is around for you when you're helpless, that defines – look, I was good at my job, right? And I loved it. I was good at taking care of my father and I *didn't* love it but if you ask me who I am, I'm not a former CEO of a successful company, I'm a woman who took care of my father.'

'And you're booked in with me, same time next week?'

Marjorie smiled, as if the abrupt ending was a game with shared rules, nodded, gathered her stuff, flailed me away from showing her out the front door and was gone. I sat on my own in the room for a long time, going back over what she had said and how she had said it, to give me a sense of what we should do with the next session. Marjorie had booked three sessions and indicated she'd come as often as needed but she was currently without income. When I went back to my office, I asked Steph to ring her and ask her to bring her CV with her next time plus an ad of any job she would think of going for, so that she could be interviewed for that job. Steph came off the phone laughing.

'She says she doesn't want effing charity,' she reported.

When Marjorie appeared, the following week, she was booted and spurred. Or at least dressed in a suit and pumps and wearing make-up. It's amazing, the difference being dressed for battle makes to someone's appearance.

'I'll get to the CV in a few. Couple of thing to be tied up from last week, first. How much do you hate your family?'

She had subtly braced herself when I mentioned the previous week but visibly relaxed when she got the question.

'I'm surprised by how little I hate them. I don't care about them. That's who they are. I don't have to choose to hang around with them. But I'm not cutting them off forever and ever or anything like that. I'm like Garfield – the orange cartoon cat? "Have a nice day – someplace else." Can't be arsed hating them. Fuck them.'

'You're glad you took your father home, you're glad you took care of him and you have somewhere to live for the next few months –'

'Happy out,' she summed it up.

'Are you?'

'Don't know. If I say I'm numb it's going to sound melodramatic but it's like when you've been for root canal. It's not sore, afterwards. You talk a bit funny but you're just numb and that's fine. Same with me. All over.'

She stood up and walked around the room, stretching. Her stretches had the flavour of a gym.

'Exactly what do you mean, "all over"?'

'I did my vomit the last day.'

'Meaning?'

'Ah, *Jasus*.'

She rolled her eyes. I waited.

'I fricking told you last week – you're the only person who's got the vomit. Haven't told anybody else in the world. None of my friends know. I needed to tell someone. I told you. End of. I mean end of. Going to stay here, get a job here. Yeah, I know, I'd be better in Australia in terms of getting a job but I don't have a mortgage or kids. I can live cheaply. I've lost a stone.'

'So I shouldn't have given you Mrs Linders's cake last week?'

'No, I've just stopped eating crap in the evening and I've been going to the gym. I let the hair grow out so I could forget roots and highlights. At some stage in the future, I will remember my father the way he was when he was himself. In the meantime, I'm going to concentrate on myself.'

'OK, let's first of all fix your CV.'

She opened her bag, took out a pad and pen and sat poised, like a secretary in an old movie.

'No specs?'

She looked blankly at me for a heartbeat, then laughed.

'I couldn't steal specs. I could steal the pad and the pen. Michael O'Leary would *so* approve.'

True enough, the pad and pen both bore the logos of hotels.

'You obviously chose your font carefully. What is it?'

'Vinderhand.'

'Get rid of it. It's pointless adolescent showoffery. Remove every adjective. Remove the reference to referees.'

'Why? Why the referees?'

'Who've you got up your sleeve?'

'My former boss in England and the man I first worked for in event management.'

'Yeah. If they want references let them ask for them. Don't announce you left your job in January, 2007. Just say you were in that job from 2000 to 2007. Then say you took a career break. One sentence. No explanation. Go on, argue with me.'

'Why should I? I'm making a big meal out of being away from the workplace by the way I'm dating it.'

'Liked the honesty of the "big thriller reader" under "Pastimes". Tidy it up and have it ready. Now, let me see the job ad. Oh, I know this company. Competitors of ours but also friends. Darcy's looking for a PA? Hmmm.'

I set up the camera, gave her a countdown and started the job interview.

Why did she want this job?

Well, it was one of the first that had caught her eye and she thought she'd be able for it.

Was she not overqualified?

Experientially, yes, but experience doesn't necessarily feed into attitude or competence.

Why had she taken a career break?

Because of a personal issue.

And, believe it or not, it went downhill from that point on.

When the recording was complete, I asked her how she thought she'd done. She silently took out the hotel pad and pen.

'So you're going to sulk at me?'

'No, I'm going to sulk at *me*. I know it was shite. Just tell me how to prevent shite and we'll be grand.'

'Telling the CEO of the company that you're going for her job because it's the first you spotted doesn't exactly endear you to her. Go research them. Find what makes them special. Find what you have that links to their special thing.'

She flagged me down with a hand and tried to write, then stopped and went back into the handbag, producing a brand new smartphone.

'Say it again and I'll record it.'

I said it again.

'Next thing – don't lecture them. You're overqualified and you want the PA job as a beginning but you really want event management, right?'

She shook her head.

'Absolute truth?'

I nodded.

'I don't know if I want to be in event management in the future. I can manage any project. I figure being PA to this woman would give me an insight into the company and all its bits and pieces and then I might stay where I was or go within the company to some other place where I knew I'd something to offer.'

'That's the answer to the "overqualified" question. Now, what's the answer to the career break question? Because it sure as hell isn't the answer you gave.'

'I took the break in order to care for my father after he had a stroke?'

'It's the truth. Why were you afraid to say that?'

'Sounded like I wasn't that committed to my career.'

'Or that you're an interesting and human person? What. You

think two and a bit years out of the workforce turns you into a knuckle-dragging moron?'

'Yep.'

'Or you think *they'll* think two and a bit years out of the workforce turns you into a knuckle-dragging moron?'

'That, too.'

Marjorie giggled. It may have been the first time in more than two years that she'd giggled.

'Yeah. I get it.'

Thirty minutes later, the recording had been completely replayed, the disc handed over and most of the hotel pad filled with notes. As the viewing of the disc progressed, she had started to spot what was wrong or missing long before I did.

'It's not all about *me*,' she summarised. 'I need to go do research on this company, on the two women who run it, on their background, etc. etc. etbloodycetera. And I hear you. I hear you. Not just website research. I need to find out who I know who knows them and find out what makes them tick so I can prove I can improve their ticking. I suppose I should come back before the interview for another go?'

'You don't need to come back. You understand exactly what you have to do and they're not going to have trick questions. They're looking for someone who can organise a clever disorganised MD. Make sure they know you're that person. That's all you have to do.'

And that's what she did. She rang me directly after the interview saying that she had performed so well they'd be stupid not to employ her. They weren't stupid.

CAREER PITFALL #10: FAMILY PROBLEMS

We now have a generation in their middle years who are caught between the demands of their own children (if they have any) and those of their parents. It's a new rendition of Tolstoy's observation that: 'Happy families are all alike; every unhappy family is unhappy in its own way.' Every family facing sudden disability in a parent or the onset of dementia must find its own way through the fresh hell either of these presents each day, week and month.

Five Tips for You as Your Own Coach

1. Decide what you're going to do as early as possible. Postponement never helps.
2. If you want to or feel you should take care of your parent for at least part of the time, check with your employer about flexitime, job-sharing or compassionate leave.
3. Check out all the support services offered by the HSE – they want to keep people in their own homes as long as possible.
4. When you're ready to go back to work, expect to experience a loss in confidence.
5. Get fit, get a new look and from that point on, concentrate, not on you but on the company where you want to work. *You* may know you've a gap in your CV but it's not so important to anyone else. People are more interested in themselves than they are in you, so join them in finding them interesting.

10

The Joy of Coaching

It's a maieutic process, coaching. Midwifery with questions. Exploration of potential, not advice. Of course, advice may come into it but when someone arrives at the beginning of the coaching process with the idea that the coach will tell them what to do, starting right there, right then, you have to tell them it's not going to be like that. They wouldn't have got to this point in their career if they didn't have brains, application and ambition, so why would they now surrender all that and let someone who hardly knows them order them around?

The sports coaches who identify and release great potential in eleven-year-olds at a soccer camp don't start with a list of ten methods each of the kids must use. That's how *bad* sporting coaches do it. The great ones watch. And then they watch some more. They watch until the mass of eager children have separated out into individuals, until they've spotted the frantic eagerness that's preventing one child from getting a feel for what's happening elsewhere on the pitch, until they have identified that another has remarkable speed and flexibility. Then they go to work developing each one.

Centuries ago, in an essay, Francis Bacon observed that 'If you would work any man, you must either know his nature and fashions and so lead him; or his ends and so persuade him; or his weaknesses and his advantages and so awe him; or those that have interest in him and so govern him.'

With the exception of the reference to governing, that's pretty much what the early days of coaching are about. Significantly, though, whereas Bacon simply assumed, based on the norms of his time, that men were the only ones to whom any of this applied, coaching, in the twenty-first century, tends to apply more to women than to men. The ratio of those taking up business coaching, in our experience, is about 70/30. More than twice as many women do it as men.

That's for a number of reasons, some of them obvious. More women are entering the workforce with higher qualifications than ever before and more of them have decided that they want to get into top management than used to be the case.

Because many businesses have been a man's world up to now, men may still be at the top and the approach and skills that worked for women at lower levels within the workforce, when the majority of their co-workers were female, need tweaking when they move to a level where the majority of their seniors and peers are male. A good coach can help a woman make that transition to top management.

Women and men alike require encouragement but it's in short supply in management, perhaps because it's in short supply in management training. Not many MBAs quote how much time they devoted, during their studies, to the importance of encouraging those who work for them. It tends to be seen either as something that will happen naturally – which it won't – or categorised as soft and fuzzy, not really important in the management scheme of things.

When I ask managers about this skill, some of them wander around the suggestion that their young graduate recruits are so confident, these days, as opposed to how they would have been twenty or thirty years ago, they hardly need encouragement. Maybe they are more confident but that doesn't mean that encouragement has been made redundant. An experiment to find out how long volunteers could stand barefoot in ice-cold water, before the bone-painful chill of it forced them to give up, found that the single most important factor in extending the length of time the water-waders could tolerate the cold was external support. When someone on dry land offered encouragement, those in the freezing water were able to extend their time substantially. Encouragement, described in the Old Testament as 'oxygen for the soul', is so rare in many workplaces that executives participating in a coaching programme often say that they look forward to their weekly or fortnightly sessions because, for the first time, they have someone who encourages them to try harder at some aspect of their daily task, has faith that they'll be able to do it, registers when they *have* done it and reinforces the process by encouragement. All of which, of course, is what management is about, but sometimes the very physical structure of a workplace militates against it. Where they can be overheard by the worker in the next cubicle, a manager is less likely to halt and praise an executive for something they have noticed has been done well but summoning the executive to the manager's office can be disruptive, disproportionate and give rise to unwelcome curiosity among colleagues.

Some multinational corporations have 'up or out' policies, which require executives to hew to a career path as upwardly slanted as Everest and in some cases (you've read Sabina's story in this book) demand that their fast-track employees gain experience in overseas plants. For single twenty-somethings, that's an opportunity of roughly equal appeal to men and women.

For twenty-somethings who have settled into parenthood, it's a very different challenge. In the old days, a stay-at-home wife might have had reservations about packing up and taking the family to wherever her husband was posted, but that's the way it worked. If the woman worked outside the home, the likelihood was that either it was a part-time job or that – even if it was full-time – she earned so much less than her mate that leaving employment in

Ireland was a sacrifice that seemed inevitable.

Today, however, the boot is often on the other foot. When the woman in a partnership is asked to spend a couple of years overseas, not only does the family get uprooted but the man faces abandoning progress – perhaps towards partnership in a legal or accountancy firm – and starting again overseas. He may also face the prospect that his wife has outpaced him in earnings and longer-term options. Making the best of this kind of barbed reality is rarely achieved by telling the man to get over it and get on with it. It can, however, be greatly helped by a coaching situation which allows either or both parties time and space free of children, each other, mobile phones, emails, deadlines and colleagues, in which to reflect, consider and explore the implications.

Six millennia back, Seneca wrote what in retrospect reads as the ultimate rationale for coaching: 'Listen to me for a day – an hour – a moment,' he begged. 'Lest I expire in my terrible wilderness, my lonely silence. O God, is there no one to listen?'

Six thousand years later, Seneca's cry echoes silently throughout Irish life. We're great communicators in this country. We can do you a mighty speech or a bit of stand-up comedy. We can sound off on radio programmes. Flip the communications coin, however, and the reality becomes clear: we're lousy listeners. We're particularly lousy listeners when it comes to listening to someone talk about themselves and spectacularly lousy listeners when it comes to hearing someone out while they talk about their problems, illness, crushed dreams or general unhappiness. The very moment someone starts to talk about any of that stuff in even a small group, watch the shutters come down.

It's not that we're not willing to help. We are, if anything, way *too* willing to help. Irish people never saw a problem they didn't want to solve by sending in the removers. An enormous range of recommendations crowds the tip of many a tongue. Recommendations like:

'You just have to complain, you can't let this continue.'

'But that's how it is.'

'You're running a temperature? God, I had flu last week and I swear to God my temperature went up to a hundred and three.'

'That's ridiculous and you're a fool if you put up with it.'

'Look, you can go the HR route or the legal route.'

Immediate recommendations to solve other people's problems ostensibly serve one need but in fact serve quite a different one. The need they're supposed to serve is that of the troubled or distressed person. The need they *actually* serve is the need of the one making the recommendation. Because a recommendation effectively sticks a sock in the complainer. If they don't do what they were advised to do, well then it's time to line up a procession of shrugs and an elevation of raised eyebrows and rolled eyes. A blunt recommendation also saves time and closes down the water-cooler conversation, which is great for the person complained to but not that helpful to the complainant, especially if the complainant is a woman.

I'm not much for the Venus/Mars portrayal of men and women as so different that it's a miracle we ever procreate, never mind work together in families and businesses, but one of the inarguable verities about a woman who expresses a doubt, worry or concern, as opposed to a man in the same situation, is that the woman doesn't want a stick-a-sock-in-it solution. Women are more likely than men to want the opportunity to explore their feelings about an issue and simply walk through the details of the narrative. In general. You noticed that qualifier? *In general,* that's the case. Some men – and, indeed, I would suggest, more men than in the past – would likewise prefer the wonderful gifts of quiet, time and attention to an instant solution forcefully supplied by a well-meaning outsider.

An encounter at work taught me, in an extremely painful manner, the importance of not offering solutions. An old friend asked to see me to discuss a problem. I welcomed her, investigated the issue, proposed the obvious remedy and saw her out, contented that I had done a stellar job. A few days later, a handwritten monogrammed card arrived from her, saying that I had lectured her the way a headmistress would. I was mortified and ashamed. I apologised at length but utterly failed to recreate the trust that had existed between us. I had been too arrogant to explore what she *wanted*. Instead, I had given her what I'd decided she *needed*. The fix was so obvious to me, I never moved beyond me to fully respect her. It wasn't that I thought I knew everything. I just thought I knew most things and that knowing things would make me useful to her.

When you're a coach, knowing stuff can be a huge disadvantage. The urge to share overcomes respect for the other person. Fortunately, I'm not completely alone in this. The next time you have a prang in your car, a virus in your person or even an item destroyed by the dry cleaner, you can check out this urge to transmit for yourself. Mention your problem in the coffee house, the office or the pub – and stand well back.

The chances are small to non-existent that any of your friends will ask you a series of questions about the issue and how you felt about it. They're much more likely to tell you how a fool T-boned them in their brand new Kia, they developed Lyme Disease because of a Californian tick or had their silk gauze permanently pleated ball gown de-pleated by the dry cleaner. Trust me. One person's problem, 90 per cent of the time, is another person's conversational starting block.

I'm not saying that coaches should be pig-ignorant. But I *am* saying that mentoring and coaching are not the same thing. Close but not identical. Mentors tend to be people who've gone and done it. They've been entrepreneurs or managing directors or product designers and are now in a position to share what they've learned with the younger generation. Coaching, on the other hand, depends much less, if at all, on passing on information, data or experience. It can be facilitated, rather than hampered, by not knowing the mechanics of someone else's trade or profession or issue.

Last year, for example, someone who works in our office came to me with a problem. A personal problem. This wasn't your minor-tiff-with-a-colleague kind of problem. This was the kind of problem that disassembles someone. Leaves them standing in the shards of what they once thought they were.

It was the kind of problem of which I had no experience. Ergo, no expertise. Therefore, no solutions to offer. Almost anybody in the office would have been better qualified to advise the individual and I was tempted to offer a list of names. (I found out later they'd talked to almost everybody else first.)

Because I was such a clean slate about this particular problem and because I had damn all to offer, I kept asking questions and listening, waiting for the metaphorical (old Edison-style) light bulb to switch on over my head, hoping for the solution to get itself into a holding pattern ready to land. No light bulb went on. No solution presented itself. Just questions. Silent presence. And – once – a mutely-offered pack of tissues. Fortunately, my friend was too occupied weeping into the tissues to notice that they had yellow smiley faces printed all over them.

The strange thing was the hug I got at the end of the couple of hours. The stranger thing was to be told that I had solved the problem. Sticking with the questions, since they'd covered a multitude up to that point, I asked about the other, much more expert friends who'd been consulted about the crisis before I was.

'Oh, they were really kind,' was the answer. 'They really were. But they were giving me advice, you know? Telling me things. They were quite right, the things they were telling me. But I didn't need *telling*. It wasn't answers I needed. I was kind of dying and I just needed to go through the process with someone who cared enough to shut the hell up.'

It was the first occasion I realized how often we see time as something to be filled, not as an asset on its own. We have more time at our disposal than any previous generation but we manage to conceal that from ourselves. We fill time with what W.B. Yeats called 'a little round of deeds and day'. To which add: solutions. Our very busy-ness rushes us to the judgment that every problem must have a solution and the more quickly we apply it, the better. Or, more frequently, the sooner the government, civil service, HSE or RSA applies the solution, the better. Because we're too busy.

We're so busy that in the evenings, what can we do but slump in front of the great time-gobbler, television. Which, of course, presents us, night after night, with enough stories of impregnable problems to give us a permanent case of compassion fatigue. Which in turn convinces us that we're suffering from dire stress and might need pharmaceutical assistance.

Even if we actually *could* find time (if we put in a bit of a search), we're reluctant to offer a listening ear – especially to an individual in trouble, partly because of personal embarrassment (OMG how will we cope with misery belonging to another soul?) but also, sometimes, because we feel unqualified to provide the right advice. Here's the good news. Mostly, humans don't want or need advice, good or bad, qualified or unqualified. What they need is time. Your time.

'Time cools, time clarifies,' Mark Twain once commented. 'No mood can be maintained quite unaltered through the course of hours.'

That's the beauty of coaching. It takes two people out of the rattling cacophony of daily life and gives them time. To think. To question. To discover strengths and ways to develop them.

It's one of the most rewarding aspects of my working life. Nothing else is as fascinating as seeing a man or woman breaking through to the best of themselves. Nothing is as rewarding as helping them get an obstacle out of their path. Nothing is as pleasurable as meeting someone years after their coaching months and learning that those months were the catalyst for a major – and comfortably achieved – career advance.

Coaches can unlock unmined potential in the people with whom they work. They can change lives for the better. That is, if they obey Goethe's great rule: 'Treat a man as he appears to be and you make him worse. But treat a man as if he already were what he potentially could be and you make him what he should be.'

Bibliography

Armstrong, Karen. *A Short History of Myth*. Canongate, 2005.

Belleret, Robert. *Piaf: Un Mythe Français*. Fayard, 2013.

Bellow, Adam. *In Praise of Nepotism*. Doubleday, 2003.

Ben-Shahar, Tal, PhD. *Happier*. McGraw-Hill, 2007.

Cain, Susan. *Quiet*. Viking Penguin, 2012.

Carr, Nicholas. *The Shallows*. Norton, 2010.

Duhigg, Charles. *The Power of Habit: Why We Do What We Do in Life and Business*. Random House, 2012.

Hammer, Professor Michael. *The Reengineering Revolution*. Harper Business, 1995.

Jaques, Elliott. *Requisite Organization: A Total System for Effective Managerial Organization and Managerial Leadership for the 21st Century*. Cason Hall & Company Publishers, 1989/2006.

Jaques, Elliott. *The Life and Behavior of Living Organisms*. Praeger, 2001.

Kahneman, Daniel. *Thinking, Fast and Slow*. Allen Lane/Penguin, 2011.

Landman, Janet. *Regret: The Persistence of the Possible*. Oxford University Press, 1993.

Maister, David, Charles H. Green and Robert M. Halford. *The Trusted Advisor*. Free Press, 2000.

Mitford, Nancy (ed.). *Noblesse Oblige: An Enquiry into the Identifiable Characteristics of the English Aristocracy* (Essays, some by Nancy Mitford). Hamish Hamilton, 1956.

Naisbitt, John. *Megatrends: Ten New Directions Transforming Our Lives*. Grand Central Publishing, 1984.

Parker, Sachi and Frederick Stroppel. *Lucky Me: My Life With – and Without – My Mom, Shirley MacLaine*. Gotham/Penguin, 2013.

Peale, Norman Vincent. *The Power of Positive Thinking*. Prentice-Hall, 1952.

Peter, Laurence J. and Raymond Hull. *The Peter Principle: Why Things Always Go Wrong*. William Morrow, 1969.

Prone, Terry. *The Fear Factor*. Londubh Books, 2011.

Trivers, Robert. *Deceit and Self-Deception: Fooling Yourself the Better to Fool Others*. Penguin, 2011.